UNITED STATES
CUSTOMS SERVICE

Importing Into the United States
A Guide for Commercial Importers

Books for Business
New York - Hong Kong

Importing Into the United States:
A Guide for Commercial Importers

by
United States Customs Service

ISBN: 0-89499-077-2

Copyright © 2001 by Books for Business

Reprinted from the 1998 edition

Books for Business
New York - Hong Kong
http://www.BusinessBooksInternational.com

In order to make original editions of historical works
available to scholars at an economical price, this
facsimile of the original edition of 1998 is
reproduced from the best available copy and has
been digitally enhanced to improve legibility, but the
text remains unaltered to retain historical
authenticity.

A NOTE TO OUR READERS

The 1998 edition of *Importing Into the United States* contains much new and revised material brought about pursuant to the Customs Modernization Act (Title VI of the North American Free Trade Agreement Implementation Act [P.L. 103-182, 107 Stat. 2057], which became effective on December 8, 1993). The Customs modernization provisions have fundamentally altered the relationship between importers and the Customs Service by shifting to the importer the legal responsibility for declaring the value, classification, and rate of duty applicable to entered merchandise.

Readers will find in this edition a new section entitled "Informed Compliance." A key component of informed compliance is the shared responsibility between Customs and the import community, wherein Customs communicates its requirements to the importer, and the importer, in turn, uses reasonable care to assure that Customs is provided accurate and timely data pertaining to his or her importations.

This publication provides an overview of the importing process and contains general information about import requirements. We have made every effort to include essential importing requirements, but it is not possible for a book this size to cover all Customs laws and regulations. Importers should also be aware that this publication does not supersede or modify any provision of those laws and regulations. Legislative and administrative changes are always under consideration and can occur at any time. Similarly, quota limitations on commodities are also subject to change.

The facts and circumstances surrounding every import transaction differ, from the experience of the importer to the nature of the imported articles. For this reason, it cannot be overemphasized that although the information in this publication is provided to promote enhanced compliance with Customs laws and regulations, the information provided is for general information purposes only. Reliance solely on the information in this publication may not be considered reasonable care.

Because a publication this size also cannot cover all the laws and regulations governing the importation of specific products, we urge interested parties to contact their nearest Customs office for information on specific issues or questions. Customs offices not listed here can be found in local telephone directories under Department of the Treasury listings. Federal agencies whose laws Customs helps to enforce are listed in the Appendix.

Importers may also wish to obtain guidance from experts in the private sector who specialize in Customs matters, for example, a licensed customs broker, attorney, or consultant. Interested parties who wish to learn more about import and export regulations, procedures and requirements, or who are interested in other Customs publications, are invited to visit our Web site at: **www.customs.ustreas.gov.**

November 1998

CONTENTS

CUSTOMS MISSION AND ORGANIZATION

1. ORGANIZATION

MISSION

The major responsibility of the U.S. Customs Service is to administer the Tariff Act of 1930, as amended. The Customs Service is one of the nation's major border enforcement agencies, so it also has responsibility for enforcing some 400 laws and regulations on international traffic and trade for 40 other government agencies. The Customs Service's mission includes: protecting the nation's revenue by assessing and collecting duties, taxes and fees incident to international traffic and trade; controlling, regulating, and facilitating the movement of carriers, people, and commodities between the United States and other nations; protecting the American consumer and the environment against the introduction of hazardous or noxious products into the United States; protecting domestic industry and labor against unfair foreign competition; and detecting, interdicting, and investigating smuggling and other illegal practices aimed at illegally entering narcotics, drugs, contraband or other prohibited articles into the United States. Customs is also responsible for detecting, interdicting, and investigating fraudulent activities intended to avoid the payment of duties, taxes and fees, or activities meant to evade the legal requirements of international traffic and trade; and for detecting, interdicting, and investigating illegal international trafficking in arms, munition and currency, and acts of terrorism at U.S. ports of entry.

ORGANIZATION

The field organization consists of 20 Customs Management Centers (CMCs), each of which is divided into service ports, area ports, and ports of entry. These organizational elements are headed, respectively, by CMC directors, service and area port directors, and port directors. Import transactions are conducted at service ports, area ports, and ports of entry, so these locations will be of primary interest to the trade community. The Customs Service is also responsible for administering the customs laws of the Virgin Islands of the United States.

SERVICE/AREA PORTS

PORT	ADDRESS	PHONE	FAX
Anchorage, AK 99501	605 W Fourth Ave	907-271-2675	907-271-2684
Atlanta, GA 30354	700 Doug Davis Dr	404-763-7020	404-763-7038
Baltimore, MD 21202	40 S. Gay St.	410-962-2666	410-962-9335
Baton Rouge, LA 70809	5353 Essen Lane	504-389-0261	504-389-0260
Blaine, WA 98230	9901 Pacific Highway	360-332-5771	360-332-4701
Boston, MA 02222-1059	10 Causeway St., Ste 603	617-565-6147	617-565-6137
Buffalo, NY 14202	111 W Huron St.	716-551-4373	716-551-5011
Calais, ME 04619	One Main St.	207-454-3621	207-454-7122
Calexico, CA 92231	P.O. Box 632	760-768-2300	760-768-2301
Champlain, NY 12919	198 West Service Rd.	518-298-8347	518-298-8314
Charleston, SC 29401	200 E Bay St	803-727-4312	803-727-4501
Charlotte, NC 28217	1901-K Cross Beam Drive	704-329-6100	704-329-6103

SERVICE/AREA PORTS—*continued*

PORT	ADDRESS	PHONE	FAX
Charlotte/Amalie, VI	Main Post Office-Sugar Estate/St Thomas, Virgin Islands 00801	809-774-2510	809-776-3489
Chicago, IL 60607-4523	610 S Canal St	312-353-6100	312-353-2337
Christiansted, VI	P.O. Box 249/St Croix, Virgin Islands 00820	809-773-1490	809-778-7419
Cleveland, OH	6747 Engle Rd Middleburg Heights, OH 44130	440-891-3800	440-891-3836
Dallas/Ft.Worth, TX	PO Box 619050 DFW Airport, TX 75261	972-574-2170	972-574-4818
Denver, CO 80239	4735 Oakland St	303-361-0712	303-361-0722
Derby Line, VT 05830	Interstate 91	802-873-3489	802-873-3628
Detroit, MI 48226	477 Michigan Ave., Suite 200	313-226-3177	313-226-3179
Douglas, AZ 85607	First St & Pan American Ave.	520-364-8486	520-364-2313
Duluth, MN 55801	515 W First St	218-720-5201	218-720-5216
El Paso, TX 79907	797 S Saragosa Rd	915-540-3025	915-540-3011
Grand Rapids, MI 49512	Kent County Airport	616-456-2515	616-285-0188
Great Falls, MT 59405	300 2nd Ave South	406-453-7631	406-453-7069
Greenville/Spartansburg, SC	150-A West Phillips Road Greer, SC 29650	864-877-8006	864-848-3454
Harrisburg, PA	Harrisburg Int'l Arpt, Bldg #135 Middletown, PA 17057-5035	717-782-4510	717-948-9294
Hartford, CT 06103	135 HighH St.	860-240-4306	860-240-4309
Highgate Springs, VT	RR 2, BOX 170 Swanton, VT 05488	802-868-2778	802-868-2373
Honolulu, HI 96813	335 Merchant St.	808-522-8060	808-522-8081
Houlton, ME 04730	RR 3 Box 5300	207-532-2131	207-532-6622
Houston/Galveston, TX	2350 N. Sam Houston Pkwy E , Ste 1000 Houston, TX 77032	281-985-6700	281-985-6706
Jacksonville, FL 32206	2831 Talleyrand Ave.	904-232-3476	904-232-1992
Kansas City, MO	2701 Rockcreek Pkwy , Ste 202 N. Kansas City, MO 64116	816-374-6439	816-374-6422
Laredo/Colombia, TX	PO Box 3130 Laredo, TX 78044	210-726-2267	210-726-2948
Los Angeles Airport Area, CA	11099 S La Cienega Blvd. Los Angeles, CA 90045	310-215-2618	310-215-2013
Los Angeles/Long Beach Seaport Area, CA	300 S. Ferry St. Terminal Island, CA 90731	310-514-6003	310-514-6769
Louisville, KY 40202	601 W Broadway	502-582-5186	502-625-7224
Miami Airport, FL	6601 W 25th St Miami, FL 33102-5280	305-869-2800	305-869-2822
Miami Seaport, FL	1500 Port Blvd Miami, FL 33132	305-536-5261	305-536-4734
Milwaukee, WI	6269 Ace Industrial Dr Cudahy, WI 53110	414-571-2860	414-762-0253
Minneapolis, MN 55401	110 S. 4th St.	612-348-1690	612-348-1630
Mobile, AL 36602	150 N. Royal St , Rm. 3004	334-441-5106	334-441-6061
Nashville, TN 37227	P.O. Box 270008	615-736-5861	615-736-5331
New Orleans, LA 70130	423 Canal St.	504-670-2391	504-670-2123
New York, NY 10048	6 World Trade Center	212-466-4444	212-466-2097
New York/JFK Area	Bldg. #77, JFK Jamaica, NY 11430	718-553-1542	718-553-0077

PORT	ADDRESS	PHONE	FAX
New York/Newark Area	Hemisphere Center, Routes 1 & 9 South Newark, NJ 07114	201-645-3760	201-645-6634
Nogales, AZ 85621	9 N Grand Ave	520-287-1410	520-287-1421
Norfolk, VA 23510	200 Granby St , Ste 839	757-441-3400	757-441-6630
Ogdensburg, NY 13669	127 N Water St	315-393-0660	315-393-7472
Orlando, FL 32827	5390 Bear Road	407-825-4300	407-648-6827
Oroville, WA 98844	Route 1, Box 130	509-476-2955	509-476-2465
Otay Mesa, CA	9777 Via De La Amistad San Diego, CA 92173	619-661-3305	619-661-3049
Pembina, ND 58271	112 W Stutsman St	701-825-6201	701-825-6473
Philadelphia, PA 19106	2nd & Chestnut Sts	215-597-4606	215-597-8370
Phoenix, AZ 85034	1315 S. 27th St	602-379-3516	602-379-3515
Port Huron, MI 48060	526 Water St	810-985-7125	810-985-3516
Portland, ME 04101	312 Fore St	207-780-3327	207-780-3420
Portland, OR 97209	511 N W Broadway, Rm 198	503-326-2865	503-326-3511
Providence, RI 02905	49 Pavilion Ave	401-941-6326	401-941-6628
Raleigh/Durham, NC	120 Southcenter Ct , Ste 500 Morrisville, NC 27560	919-467-3552	919-467-0706
Richmond, VA 23231	4501 Wmsburg Rd, Ste G	804-226-9675	804-226-1197
San Antonio, TX 78216	9800 Airport Blvd	210-821-6965	210-821-6968
San Francisco, CA 94105	555 Battery St	415-782-9200	415-774-7710
San Juan, PR 00901	Number One La Puntilla	787-729-6850	787-729-6678
San Luis, AZ 85349	P.O Box H	520-627-8854	520-627-9850
San Ysidro, CA 92073	720 E San Ysidro Blvd	619-662-7201	619-622-7374
Sault Ste. Marie, MI 49783	Intl Bridge Plaza	906-632-7221	906-632-6171
Savannah, GA 31401	1 East Bay St	912-652-4256	912-652-4435
Seattle, WA 98104- 1049	1000 2nd Ave, Ste 2100	206-553-0770	206-553-2940
St Albans, VT 05478	P.O. Box 1490	802-524-6527	802-527-1338
St. Louis, MO 63134	4477 Woodson Rd	314-428-2662	314-428-2889
Syracuse, NY	4034 S. Service Rd N. Syracuse, NY 13212	315-455-2271	315-455-7512
Tacoma, WA 98421	2202 Port of Tacoma Rd	206-593-6336	206-593-6351
Tampa, FL 33605	1624 E. Seventh Ave , Ste 101	813-228-2385	813-225-7309
Tucson, AZ 85706	7150 S. Tucson Blvd.	520-670-6461	520-670-6648
Washington, DC 20041	PO Box 17423	703-318-5900	703-318-6706
Wilmington, NC 28401	One Virginia Ave	910-815-4601	910-815-4581

PORTS OF ENTRY BY STATE (Including Puerto Rico and the U.S. Virgin Islands)

ALABAMA
Birmingham
Huntsville
Mobile

ALASKA
Alcan
Anchorage
Dalton Cache
Fairbanks
Juneau
Ketchikan
Kodiak
Sitka
Skagway
Valdez
Wrangell

ARIZONA
Douglas
Lukeville
Naco
Nogales
Phoenix
San Luis
Sasabe
Tucson

ARKANSAS
Little Rock-N Little Rock

CALIFORNIA
Andrade
Calexico
Eureka
Fresno
Los Angeles-Long Beach
Port San Luis
San Diego
San Francisco-Oakland
Tecate
San Ysidro-Otay Mesa

COLORADO
Denver

CONNECTICUT
Bridgeport
Hartford
New Haven
New London

DELAWARE
Wilmington/Chester

DISTRICT OF COLUMBIA
Dulles Airport

FLORIDA
Fernandina Beach
Jacksonville
Key West
Miami
Orlando
Panama City
Pensacola
Port Canaveral
Port Everglades
Port Manatee
St Petersburg
Tampa
West Palm Beach

GEORGIA
Atlanta
Brunswick

HAWAII
Honolulu
Hilo
Kahului
Nawiliwili-Port Allen

IDAHO
Boise
Eastport
Porthill

ILLINOIS
Chicago
Peoria
Rock Island-Moline*
   (See Davenport, Iowa)

INDIANA
Evansville/Owensboro, Ky
Indianapolis
Lawrenceburg/
   Cincinnati, Ohio

IOWA
Davenport-Rock Island
   Moline*
Des Moines

KANSAS
Wichita

KENTUCKY
Louisville
Owensboro/Evansville, Ind

LOUISIANA
Baton Rouge
Gramercy
Lake Charles
Morgan City
New Orleans
Shreveport/Bossier City

MAINE
Bangor
Bar Harbor
Bath
Belfast
Bridgewater
Calais

Eastport
Fort Fairfield
Fort Kent
Houlton
Jackman
Jonesport
Limestone
Madawaska
Portland
Rockland
Van Buren
Vanceboro

MARYLAND
Baltimore/Annapolis/
   Cambridge

MASSACHUSETTS
Boston
Fall River
Gloucester
Lawrence
New Bedford
Plymouth
Salem
Springfield
Worcester

MICHIGAN
Battle Creek
Detroit
Grand Rapids
Muskegon
Port Huron
Saginaw-Bay City/Flint
Sault Ste. Marie

MINNESOTA
Baudette
Duluth and Superior, Wis
Grand Portage
International Falls-Ranier
Minneapolis-St Paul
Noyes
Pinecreek
Roseau
Warroad

MISSISSIPPI
Greenville
Gulfport
Jackson
Pascagoula
Vicksburg

MISSOURI
Kansas City
St. Joseph
St Louis
Springfield

MONTANA
Butte
Del Bonita
Great Falls
Morgan
Opheim
Piegan
Raymond
Roosville

Scobey
Sweetgrass
Turner
Whitetail
Whitlash

NEBRASKA
Omaha

NEVADA
Las Vegas
Reno

NEW HAMPSHIRE
Portsmouth

NEW JERSEY
Perth Amboy (See
   New York/Newark)

NEW MEXICO
Albuquerque
Columbus
Santa Teresa

NEW YORK
Albany
Alexandria Bay
Buffalo-Niagara Falls
Cape Vincent
Champlain-Rouses Point
Clayton
Massena
New York
   Kennedy Airport Area
   Newark Area
   New York Seaport Area
Ogdensburg
Rochester/Sodus Point
Syracuse/Utica/Oswego
Trout River/Chateaugay/Fort
   Covington

NORTH CAROLINA
Beaufort-Morehead City
Charlotte
Durham
Reidsville
Wilmington
Winston-Salem

NORTH DAKOTA
Ambrose
Antler
Carbury
Dunseith
Fortuna
Hannah
Hansboro
Maida
Neche
Noonan
Northgate
Pembina
Portal
Sarles
Sherwood
St John
Walhalla
Westhope

OHIO
Ashtabula/Conneaut
Cincinnati/
   Lawrenceburg, Ind
Cleveland/Akron
Columbus
Dayton
Toledo/Sandusky

OKLAHOMA
Oklahoma City
Tulsa

OREGON
Astoria*
Coos Bay
Newport
Portland*

PENNSYLVANIA
Chester (See Phila)
Erie
Harrisburg
Lee Valley
Philadelphia
Pittsburgh
Wilkes-Barre/Scranton

PUERTO RICO
Aguadilla
Fajardo
Guanica
Humacao
Jobos
Mayaguez
Ponce
San Juan

RHODE ISLAND
Newport
Providence

SOUTH CAROLINA
Charleston
Columbia
Georgetown
Greenville-Spartanburg

SOUTH DAKOTA
Sioux Falls

TENNESSEE
Chattanooga
Knoxville
Memphis
Nashville

TEXAS
Amarillo
Austin
Brownsville
Corpus Christi
Dallas/Ft Worth
Del Rio
Eagle Pass
El Paso
Fabens
Freeport
Hidalgo
Houston/Galveston

Laredo
Lubbock
Orange* (Beaumont)
Port Arthur/Sabine*
Port Lavaca-Point Comfort
Presidio
Progreso
Rio Grande City
Roma
San Antonio

UTAH
Salt Lake City

VERMONT
Beecher Falls
Burlington
Derby Line
Highgate Springs/Alburg
Norton
Richford
St Albans

VIRGIN ISLANDS
Charlotte Amalie,
   St Thomas
Christiansted
Coral Bay
Cruz Bay
Frederiksted

VIRGINIA
Alexandria
Norfolk-Newport News
Richmond-Petersburg

WASHINGTON
Aberdeen
Anacortes*
Bellingham*
Blaine
Boundary (Frontier)
Danville
Everett*

Ferry
Friday Harbor*
Frontier
Laurier
Longview*
Lynden
Metaline Falls
Neah Bay* (Port Angeles)
Nighthawk
Olympia* (Tacoma)
Oroville
Point Roberts
Port Angeles*
Port Townsend*
Seattle*
Spokane
Sumas
Tacoma*

WEST VIRGINIA
Charleston

WISCONSIN
Ashland
Green Bay
Manitowoc (Milwaukee)
Marinette (Milwaukee)
Milwaukee
Racine
Sheboygan (Milwaukee)

* Consolidated Ports
  Columbia River port includes Longview, WA, and Astoria and Portland, OR.
  Beaumont, Orange, Port Arthur, Sabine port of entry includes ports of the same name
  Port of Puget Sound includes Tacoma, Seattle, Port Angeles, Port Townsend, Neah Bay, Friday Harbor, Everett, Bellingham,
     Anacortes, and Olympia in the State of Washington.
  Port of Rock Island includes Moline and Davenport, IA
  Port of Shreveport includes Bossier City, LA
  Designated user-fee airports Fargo, ND, Ft Myers, FL, Ft Wayne, IN; Jackson, MS, Klamath County, OR, Lebanon, NH, Lexington,
     KY, Midland, TX, Morristown, NJ, Oakland-Pontiac, MI, Rockford, IL, Sanford, FL, St Paul, AK; Waukegan, IL; Wilmington, OH;
     Yakima, WA

CUSTOMS MANAGEMENT CENTERS

ARIZONA
4740 North Oracle Rd.
Tucson, AZ 85705
520-670-5900
Fax 670-5911

CARIBBEAN AREA
#1 La Puntilla St
San Juan, PR 00901
787-729-6950
Fax 729-6978

EAST GREAT LAKES
4455 Genesee St
Buffalo, NY 14225
716-626-0400
Fax 626-1164

EAST TEXAS
2323 S Shepard St.
Houston, TX 77019
713-313-2843
Fax 313-2849

GULF
423 Canal St
New Orleans, LA 70130
504-670-2404
Fax 670-2286

MID AMERICA
610 S Canal St
Chicago, Il 60607
312-353-4733
Fax 886-4921

MID ATLANTIC
103 S Gay St
Baltimore, MD 21202
410-962-6200
Fax 962-2449

MID PACIFIC
33 New Montgomery St
San Francisco, CA 94105
415-744-1530
Fax 744-7005

NEW YORK
6 World Trade Center
New York, NY 10048
212-466-4444
Fax 466-2097

NORTH ATLANTIC
10 Causeway St
Boston, MA 02222
617-565-6210
Fax 565-6277

NORTH FLORIDA
1624 E Seventh Ave.
Tampa Fl 33605
813-228-2381
Fax 228-7110

NORTH PACIFIC
511 N W Broadway
Portland, OR 97209
503-326-7625
Fax 326-7629

**NORTHWEST GREAT
PLAINS**
1000 Second Ave.
Seattle, Wa 98104
206-553-6944
Fax 553-1401

SOUTH ATLANTIC
161 Phoenix Blvd.
College Park, GA 30349
770-994-2306
Fax 994-2315

SOUTH FLORIDA
909 SE First Ave
Miami, FL 33131
305-536-6600
Fax 536-6752

SOUTH PACIFIC
One World Trade Center
PO Box 32639
Long Beach, CA 90815
562-980-3100
Fax 980-3107

SOUTH TEXAS
PO Box 3130, Bldg #2
Lincoln-Juarez Bridge
Laredo, TX 78044
210-718-4161
Fax 794-1015

SOUTHERN CALIFORNIA
610 W. Ash St.
San Diego, CA 92101
619-557-5455
Fax 557-5394

WEST GREAT LAKES
613 Abbott St.
Detroit, MI 48226
313-226-2955
Fax 226-3118

WEST TEXAS/NEW MEXICO
9400 Viscount Blvd.
El Paso, TX 79925
915-540-5800
Fax 540-5792

U.S. CUSTOMS OFFICERS IN FOREIGN COUNTRIES

AUSTRIA
Customs Attaché
American Embassy
Boltzmanngasse 16
A-1091 Vienna
Tel: 43-1-313-39-2112

BELGIUM
U S Mission to the
European Communities
B-100
Brussels
Tel 508-4378

CANADA
Customs Attaché
American Embassy
100 Wellington St
Ottawa, Ontario
K1P 5T1
Tel. (613) 238-4470 Ext 322

CENTRAL AMERICA
Customs Attaché
Central America
10300 Sunset Drive
Suite 380
Miami, FL 33173-3038
Tel 305-596-6405

CHINA
Customs Attaché
American Embassy
Beijing, Peoples' Republic
Tel 10-6500-3049

FRANCE
Customs Attaché
American Embassy
58 bis Rue la Boetie
75008 Paris
Tel 331-4312-7400

GERMANY
Customs Attaché
American Embassy
Deichmanns Aue 29
35170 Bonn
Tel 228-339-2207

U S Customs Service
American Consulate
Platenstrasse 9
60320 Frankfurt AM Main
Tel 69-7535-3630

HONG KONG
American Consulate General
26 Garden Road
Room 221
Central Hong Kong
Tel 2524-2267

ITALY
Customs Attaché
American Embassy
Via Veneto 119
00187 Rome
Tel 6-4674-2475

Sr Customs Representative
American Consulate General
Via Principe Amedeo, 2/10
20121 Milan
Tel: 2-29035-218

JAPAN
Customs Attaché
American Embassy
10-5, Akasaka 1-Chome
Minato-ku
Tokyo 107
Tel 81-3-3224-5433

KOREA
Customs Attaché
82 SeJong-Ro
Chongro-Ku
Seoul 110-050
Tel 397-4644

MEXICO
Sr. Customs Representative
American Consulate General
No 139 Morelia
Hermosillo, Sonora
Tel 62-17-5741

Customs Attaché
American Embassy
Paseo de la Reforma 305
Colonia Cuauhtemoc
Mexico City, D.F
Tel 209-9100

Sr Customs Representative
American Consulate
Paseo Montejo 453
Merida, Yucatan 97000
Tel 99-25-8235

Sr Customs Representative
American Consulate General
Avenida Constitucion
411 Poniente
Monterrey Mexico, N L
Tel 342-7972

THE NETHERLANDS
Customs Attaché
American Embassy
Lange Voorhout 102
2514EJ The Hague
Tel: 703-924-651

PANAMA
Customs Attaché
American Embassy
Calle 38 & Avenida Balboa
Panama, City
Tel 507-225-7562

RUSSIA
Customs Attaché
American Embassy
19-23 Novinsky Blvd
Moscow 121099
Tel 095-956-4417

SINGAPORE
Customs Attaché
American Embassy
27 Napier Road
Singapore 258508
Tel. 476-9275

SOUTH AFRICA
Customs Attaché
American Embassy
895 Schoemann Street
Arcadia, Pretoria 0001
Tel: 12-342-8062

THAILAND
Customs Attaché
American Embassy
120 Wireless Road
Bangkok
Tel 205-5015

UNITED KINGDOM
Customs Attaché
American Embassy
24/31 Grosvenor Square
London, W1A 1AE
Tel. 171-493-4599

URUGUAY
Customs Attaché
American Embassy
1776 Lauro Muller
Montevideo
Tel: 598-2401-1835

VENEZUELA
Customs Attaché
American Embassy
Calle B con Calle F
Colinas de Valle Arriba
Caracas
Tel. 2-977-4594

SUGGESTIONS TO THE EXPORTER

FOR FASTER CUSTOMS CLEARANCE:

1.   Include all information required on your Customs invoices.

2.   Prepare your invoices carefully. Type them clearly. Allow sufficient space between lines. Keep the data within each column.

3.   Make sure that your invoices contain the information that would be shown on a well-prepared packing list.

4.   Mark and number each package so that it can be identified with the corresponding marks and numbers appearing on your invoice.

5.   Show on your invoice a detailed description of each item of merchandise contained in each individual package.

6.   Mark your goods legibly and conspicuously with the name of the country of origin, unless they are specifically exempted from the country-of-origin marking requirements, and with such other marking as required by the marking laws of the United States. Exemptions and general marking requirements are detailed in Chapters 29 and 30.

7.   Comply with the provisions of any special laws of the United States which may apply to your goods, such as the laws relating to food, drugs, cosmetics, alcoholic beverages, radioactive materials, and others. (See Chapters 33, 34 and 35.)

8.   Observe closely the instructions with respect to invoicing, packaging, marking, labeling, etc., sent to you by your customer in the United States. He or she has probably made a careful check of the requirements which will have to be met when your merchandise arrives.

9.   Work with U.S. Customs in developing packing standards for your commodities.

10. Establish sound security procedures at your facility and while transporting your goods for shipment. Do not give narcotics smugglers the opportunity to introduce narcotics into your shipment.

11. Consider shipping on a carrier participating in the Automated Manifest System.

12. If you use a licensed customs broker to handle the transaction, consider using a firm that participates in the Automated Broker Interface (ABI).

2. ENTRY PROCESS

When a shipment reaches the United States, the importer of record (i.e., the owner, purchaser, or licensed customs broker designated by the owner, purchaser, or consignee) will file entry documents for the goods with the port director at the port of entry. Imported goods are not legally entered until after the shipment has arrived within the port of entry, delivery of the merchandise has been authorized by Customs, and estimated duties have been paid. It is the responsibility of the importer of record to arrange for examination and release of the goods.

Pursuant to 19 U.S.C. 1484, the importer of record must use reasonable care in making entry.

NOTE: In addition to contacting the U.S. Customs Service, importers should contact other agencies when questions arise regarding particular commodities. For example, questions about products regulated by the Food and Drug Administration should be forwarded to the nearest FDA district office (check local phone book under U.S. Government listings) or to the Import Division, FDA Headquarters, (301) 443-6553. The same is true for alcohol, tobacco, firearms, wildlife products (furs, skins, shells), motor vehicles, and other products and merchandise regulated by the other federal agencies for which Customs enforces entry laws. Appropriate agencies are identified in Chapter 33.

Addresses and phone numbers for these agencies are listed in the appendix.

Goods may be entered for consumption, entered for warehouse at the port of arrival, or they may be transported in-bond to another port of entry and entered there under the same conditions as at the port of arrival. Arrangements for transporting the merchandise to an interior port in-bond may be made by the consignee, by a customs broker, or by any other person having a sufficient interest in the goods for that purpose. Unless your merchandise arrives directly at the port where you wish to enter it, you may be charged additional fees by the carrier for transportation to that port unless other arrangements have been made. Under some circumstances, your goods may be released through your local Customs port even though they arrive at another port from a foreign country. Arrangements must be made prior to arrival at the Customs port where you intend to file your duties and documentation.

Goods to be placed in a foreign trade zone are not entered at the customs house. See Chapter 38 for further information.

EVIDENCE OF RIGHT TO MAKE ENTRY

Goods may be entered only by the owner, purchaser, or by a licensed customs broker. When the goods are consigned "to order," the bill of lading, properly endorsed by the consignor, may serve as evidence of the right to make entry. An air waybill may be used for merchandise arriving by air.

In most instances, entry is made by a person or firm certified by the carrier bringing the goods to the port of entry. This entity is considered the "owner" of the goods for customs purposes. The document issued by the carrier is known as a "Carrier's Certificate." An example of this certificate is shown in the Appendix. In certain circumstances, entry may be made by means of a duplicate bill of lading or a shipping receipt. When the goods are not imported by a common carrier, possession of the goods by the importer at the time of arrival shall be deemed sufficient evidence of the right to make entry.

ENTRY FOR CONSUMPTION

The entry of merchandise is a two-part process consisting of (1) filing the documents necessary to determine whether merchandise may be released from Customs custody, and (2) filing the documents which contain information for duty assessment and statistical purposes. Both of these processes can be accomplished electronically via the Automated Broker Interface (ABI) program of the Automated Commercial Systems.

ENTRY DOCUMENTS

Within five working days of the date of a shipment's arrival at a U.S. port of entry, entry documents must be filed at a location specified by the port director, unless an extension is granted. These documents consist of:

- Entry Manifest (Customs Form 7533) or Application and Special Permit for Immediate Delivery (Customs Form 3461) or other form of merchandise release required by the port director.

- Evidence of right to make entry.

- Commercial invoice or a pro forma invoice when the commercial invoice cannot be produced.

- Packing lists if appropriate.

- Other documents necessary to determine merchandise admissibility.

If the goods are to be released from Customs custody on entry documents, an entry summary for consumption must be filed and estimated duties deposited at the port of entry within 10 working days of the time the goods are entered.

SURETY

The entry must be accompanied by evidence that bond is posted with Customs to cover any potential duties, taxes, and charges that may accrue. Bonds may be secured through a resident U.S. surety company but may be posted in the form of United States money or certain United States government obligations. In the event that a customs broker is employed for the purpose of making entry, the broker may permit the use of his bond to provide the required coverage.

ENTRY SUMMARY DOCUMENTATION

Following presentation of the entry, the shipment may be examined, or examination may be waived. The shipment is then released provided no legal or regulatory violations have occurred. Entry summary documentation is filed and estimated duties are deposited within 10 working days of the entry of the merchandise at a designated customs house. Entry summary documentation consists of:

- The entry package returned to the importer, broker, or his authorized agent after merchandise is permitted release.

- Entry summary (Customs Form 7501).

- Other invoices and documents necessary for the assessment of duties, collection of statistics, or the determination that all import requirements have been satisfied. This paper documentation can be reduced or eliminated when utilizing features of the ABI.

IMMEDIATE DELIVERY

An alternate procedure which provides for immediate release of a shipment may be used in some cases by making application for a special permit for immediate delivery on Customs Form 3461 prior to the arrival of the merchandise. Carriers participating in the Automated Manifest System can receive conditional release authorizations after leaving the foreign country and up to five days before landing in the United States. If the application is approved, the shipment is released expeditiously following arrival. An entry summary must then be filed in proper form, either on paper or electronically, and estimated duties deposited within 10 working days of release. Immediate-delivery release using Form 3461 is limited to the following types of merchandise:

- Merchandise arriving from Canada or Mexico, if approved by the port director and an appropriate bond is on file.

- Fresh fruits and vegetables for human consumption arriving from Canada or

Mexico and removed from the area immediately contiguous to the border to the importer's premises within the port of importation.

- Shipments consigned to or for the account of any agency or officer of the U.S. government.

- Articles for a trade fair.

- Tariff-rate quota merchandise and, under certain circumstances, merchandise subject to an absolute quota. Absolute quota items require a formal entry at all times.

- In very limited circumstances, merchandise released from warehouse followed within 10 working days by a warehouse withdrawal for consumption.

- Merchandise specifically authorized by Customs Headquarters to be entitled to release for immediate delivery.

ENTRY FOR WAREHOUSE

If it is desired to postpone release of the goods, they may be placed in a Customs bonded warehouse under a warehouse entry. The goods may remain in the bonded warehouse up to five years from the date of importation. At any time during that period, warehoused goods may be reexported without the payment of duty, or they may be withdrawn for consumption upon the payment of duty at the rate of duty in effect on the date of withdrawal. If the goods are destroyed under Customs supervision, no duty is payable.

While the goods are in the bonded warehouse, they may, under Customs supervision, be manipulated by cleaning, sorting, repacking, or otherwise changing their condition by processes which do not amount to manufacturing. After manipulation and within the warehousing period, the goods may be exported without the payment of duty, or they may be withdrawn for consumption upon payment of duty at the rate applicable to the goods in their manipulated condition at the time of withdrawal. Perishable goods, explosive substances, or prohibited importations may not be placed in a bonded warehouse. Certain restricted articles, though not allowed release from custody, may be warehoused.

Information regarding bonded manufacturing warehouses is contained in section 311 of the Tariff Act (19 U.S.C. 1311).

UNENTERED GOODS

If there is a failure to file an entry for the goods at the port of entry, or at the port of destination for in-bond shipments, within five working days after their arrival, the goods may be place in a general-order warehouse at the importer's risk and expense. If the goods are not entered within six months from the date of importation, they can be sold at public auction. Perishable goods, goods subject to depreciation, and explosive substances, however, may be sold sooner.

Storage charges, expenses of sales, internal revenue or other taxes, duties, fees, and amounts for the satisfaction of liens must be taken out of the money obtained from the sale of the unentered goods. Any surplus remaining after these deductions is ordinarily payable to the holder of a duly endorsed bill of lading covering the goods if a claim is made within 10 days of the sale. Carriers, not port directors, are required to notify a bonded warehouse of unentered merchandise. Once notified, the bonded warehouse operator/manager shall arrange for the unentered merchandise to be transported to his or her premises for storage at the consignee's risk and expense. If the goods are subject to internal revenue taxes and will not bring enough to pay the taxes if sold at public auction, they are subject to destruction.

MAIL ENTRIES

Importers have found that in some cases it is to their advantage to use the mails to import merchandise into the United States. Some benefits to be gained are:

- Ease in clearing shipments through Customs. The duties on parcels valued at $2,000 or less are collected by the letter carrier who delivers the parcel to the addressee (see note below).

- Savings on shipping charges. Smaller, low-valued packages can often be sent less expensively through the mails.

- No formal entry required on duty-free merchandise not exceeding $2,000 in value.
- No need to clear shipments personally if under $2,000 in value.

Joint Customs and postal regulations provide that all parcel post packages must have a Customs declaration securely attached to the outer wrapping giving an accurate description of the contents and their value. This declaration is obtained at post offices worldwide. Commercial shipments must also be accompanied by a commercial invoice enclosed in the parcel bearing the declaration.

Each mail parcel containing an invoice or statement of value should be marked on the outer wrapper, on the address side, "Invoice enclosed." If the invoice or statement cannot be conveniently enclosed within the sealed parcel, it may be securely attached to the parcel. Failure to comply with any of these requirements will delay clearance of the shipment through Customs.

Packages other than parcel post, like letter-class mail, commercial papers, printed matter, or samples of merchandise, must bear on the address side a label, Form C1, provided by the Universal Post Union, or the endorsement "May be opened for customs purposes before delivery," or similar words definitely waiving the privacy of the seal and indicating that Customs officers may open the parcel without recourse to the addressee. Parcels not labeled or endorsed in this manner and found to contain prohibited merchandise or merchandise subject to duty or tax are subject to forfeiture.

A Customs officer prepares the Customs entry for mail importations not exceeding $2,000 in value, and the letter carrier at the destination delivers the parcel to the addressee upon payment of the duty. If the value of a mail importation exceeds $2,000, the addressee is notified to prepare and file a formal Customs entry (also called a consumption entry) for it at the Customs port nearest him. A commercial invoice is required with the entry.

A Customs processing fee of $5.00 will be assessed on each item of dutiable mail for which a Customs officer prepares documentation. This nominal charge on all dutiable or taxable mail, in addition to the duty, is collected by the postal carrier. There is also a postal fee (in addition to prepaid postage) authorized by international postal conventions and agreements as partial reimbursement to the Postal Service for its work in clearing packages through Customs and delivering them.

NOTE: The following general exceptions apply to the $2,000 limit:

Articles classified in Subchapters III and IV, Chapter 99, HTSUS	Leather, articles of
Billfolds and other flat goods	Luggage
Feathers and feather products	Millinery ornaments
Flowers and foliage, artificial or preserved	Pillows and cushions
Footwear	Plastics, miscellaneous articles of
Fur, articles of	Rawhides and skins
Gloves	Rubber, miscellaneous articles of
Handbags	Textile fibers and products
Headwear and hat braids	Toys, games, and sports equipment
	Trimmings

The limit for these articles is $250, except for textiles (fibers and products), virtually all commercial shipments of which require formal entry, regardless of value. Unaccompanied shipments of made-to-measure suits from Hong Kong, which includes single suits for personal consumption, also require a formal entry regardless of the suit's value.

---

3. RIGHT TO MAKE ENTRY

ENTRY BY IMPORTER

Merchandise arriving in the United States by commercial carrier must be entered by the owner, purchaser, his or her authorized regular employee, or by the licensed customs broker designated by the owner, purchaser, or consignee. U.S. Customs officers and employees are not authorized to act as agents for importers or forwarders of imported merchandise, although they may give all reasonable advice and assistance to inexperienced importers.

Customs brokers are the only persons who are authorized by the tariff laws of the United States to act as agents for importers in the transaction of their customs business. Customs brokers are private individuals or firms licensed by the Customs Service to prepare and file the necessary Customs entries, arrange for the payment of duties found due, take steps to effect the release of the goods in Customs custody, and otherwise represent their principals in customs matters. The fees charged for these services may vary according to the customs broker and the extent of services performed.

Every entry must be supported by one of the forms of evidence of the right to make entry outlined in this chapter. When entry is made by a customs broker, a Customs power of attorney is made in the name of the customs broker. This power of attorney is given by the person or firm for whom the customs broker is acting as agent. Ordinarily, the authority of an employee to make entry for his or her employer is established most satisfactorily by a Customs power of attorney.

ENTRIES MADE BY OTHERS

Entry of goods may be made by a nonresident individual or partnership, or by a foreign corporation through a U.S. agent or representative of the exporter, a member of the partnership, or an officer of the corporation.

The surety on any Customs bond required from a nonresident individual or organization must be incorporated in the United States. In addition, a foreign corporation in whose name merchandise is entered must have a resident agent in the state where the port of entry is located who is authorized to accept service of process in the foreign corporation's behalf.

A licensed customs broker named in a Customs power of attorney may make entry on behalf of the exporter or his representative. The owner's declaration made by a nonresident individual or organization which the customs broker may request must be supported by a surety bond providing for the payment of increased or additional duties found due. Liability for duties is discussed in Chapter 13. An owner's declaration executed in a foreign country is acceptable, but it must be executed before a notary public and bear the notary's seal. Notaries public will be found in all American embassies around the world and in most of the larger consulates.

POWER OF ATTORNEY

A nonresident individual, partnership, or foreign corporation may issue a power of attorney to a regular employee, customs broker, partner, or corporation officer to act in the United States for the nonresident employer. Any person named in a power of attorney must be a resident of the United States who has been authorized to accept service of process on behalf of the person or organization issuing the power of attorney. The power of attorney to accept service of process becomes irrevocable with respect to Customs transactions duly undertaken. Either the applicable Customs form (see Appendix) or a document using the same language as the form is acceptable. References to acts which the issuer has not authorized the agent to perform may be deleted from the form or omitted from the document. A power of attorney from a foreign corporation must be supported by the following documents or their equivalent when foreign law or practice differs from that in the United States:

- A certificate from the proper public officer of the country showing the legal existence of the corporation, unless the fact of incorporation is so generally known as to be a matter of common knowledge.

- A copy of that part of the charter or articles of incorporation which shows the scope of the corporation's business and its governing body.

- A copy of the document or part thereof by which the person signing the power of attorney derives his authority, such as a provision of the charter or articles of incorporation, a copy of the resolution, minutes of the board of directors' meeting, or other document by which the governing body conferred this authority. In this case a copy is required of the bylaws or other document giving the governing board the authority to designate others to appoint agents or attorney.

A nonresident individual or partnership or a foreign corporation may issue a power of attorney to authorize the persons or firms named in the power of attorney to issue like powers of attorney to other qualified residents of the United States and to empower the residents to whom such powers of attorney are issued to accept service of process on behalf of the nonresident individual or organizations.

A power of attorney issued by a partnership must be limited to a period not to exceed two years from the date of execution and shall state the names of all members of the partnership. One member of a partnership may execute a power of attorney for the transaction of customs business of the partnership. When a new firm is formed by a change of membership, the prior firm's power of attorney is no longer effective for any customs purpose. The new firm will be required to issue a new power of attorney for the transaction of its customs business. All other powers of attorney may be granted for an unlimited period.

Customs Form 5291, or a document using the same language as the form, is also used to empower an agent other than an attorney-at-law or customs broker to file protests on behalf of an importer under section 514 of the Tariff Act of 1930 as amended. (See 19 CFR 141.32.)

Foreign corporations may comply with Customs regulations by executing a power of attorney on the corporation's letterhead. A form of power of attorney used for this purpose is given below. A nonresident individual or partner may use this same form.

The X Corporation,_____
(Address, city, and country)

organized under the laws of_____hereby authorizes

_____
(Name or names of employee or officer in United States)

_____
(and address or addresses)

to perform on behalf of the said corporation any and all acts specified in Customs Form 5291, Power of Attorney; to accept service of process in the United States on behalf of the X Corporation; to issue powers of attorney on Customs Form 5291 authorizing a qualified resident or residents of the United States to perform on behalf of the X Corporation all acts specified in Customs Form 5291; and to empower such resident or residents to accept service of process in the United States on behalf of the said X Corporation.

Because the laws regarding incorporation, notation, and authentication of documents vary from country to country, the agent to be named in the power of attorney should consult the port director of Customs at the port of entry where proof of the document's existence may be required as to the proper form to be used and the formalities to be met.

4. EXAMINATION OF GOODS AND ENTRY DOCUMENTS

Examination of goods and documents is necessary to determine, among other things:

- The value of the goods for customs purposes and their dutiable status.

- Whether the goods must be marked with their country of origin or require special marking or labeling. If so, whether they are marked in the manner required.

- Whether the shipment contains prohibited articles.

- Whether the goods are correctly invoiced.

- Whether the goods are in excess of the invoiced quantities or a shortage exists.

- Whether the shipment contains illegal narcotics.

Prior to the goods' release, the port director will designate representative quantities for examination by Customs officers under conditions that will safeguard the goods. Some kinds of goods must be examined to determine whether they meet special requirements of the law. For example, food and beverages unfit for human consumption would not meet the requirements of the Food and Drug Administration.

One of the primary methods of smuggling narcotics into the United States is in cargo shipments. Drug smugglers will place narcotics inside a legitimate cargo shipment or container to be retrieved upon arrival in the United States. Because smugglers use any means possible to hide narcotics, all aspects of the shipment are examined, including container, pallets, boxes, and product. Only through intensive inspection can narcotics be discovered.

Textiles and textile products are considered trade-sensitive and as such may be subject to a higher percentage of examinations than other commodities.

Customs officers will ascertain the quantity of goods imported, making allowances for shortages under specified conditions and assessing duty on any excess. The invoice may state the quantities in the weights and measures of the country from which the goods are shipped or in the weights and measures of the United States, but the entry must state the quantities in metric terms.

EXCESS GOODS AND SHORTAGES

In order to facilitate duty allowances for goods that do not arrive and to determine whether excess goods are contained in the shipment, the importer (or foreign exporter) is advised to pack the goods in an orderly fashion; properly mark and number the packages in which the goods are contained; list each package's contents on the invoice; and place marks and numbers on the invoices that correspond to those packages.

If the Customs officer finds any package that contains an article not specified on the invoice, and there is reason to believe the article was omitted from the invoice by fraud, gross negligence or negligence on the part of the seller, shipper, owner or agent, a monetary penalty may be imposed, or in some cases, the merchandise may be seized or forfeited. (See e.g., 19 U.S.C. 1592.)

If, during the examination of any package that has been designated for examination, the Customs officer finds a deficiency in quantity, weight or measure, he or she will make a duty allowance for the deficiency. An allowance in duty may be made for those packages not designated as long as the importer notifies the port director of the shortage before liquidation of the entry becomes final and establishes to the port director's satisfaction that the missing goods were not delivered.

DAMAGE OR DETERIORATION

Goods that the Customs officer finds to be entirely without commercial value at the time of arrival in the United States because of damage or deterioration are treated as a "nonimportation." No duties are assessed on these goods.

When damage or deterioration is present with respect to part of the shipment only, allowance in duties is not made unless the importer segregates, under Customs supervision, the damaged or deteriorated part from the remainder of the shipment. When the shipment consists of fruits, vegetables, or other perishable merchandise, allowance in duties cannot be made unless the importer, within 96 hours of unloading the merchandise and before it has been removed from the pier, files an application for an allowance with the port director. Allowance or reduction of duty for partial damage or loss as a result of rust or discoloration is precluded by law on shipments consisting of any article partially or wholly manufactured of iron or steel, or any manufacture of iron or steel.

TARE

In determining the quantity of goods dutiable on net weight, a deduction is made from the gross weight for just and reasonable tare. *Tare* is the allowance for a deficiency in the weight or quantity of the merchandise caused by the weight of the box, cask, bag, or other receptacle that contains the merchandise and that is weighed with it. The following schedule tares are provided for in the Customs Regulations:

Apple boxes. 3.6 kilograms (8 lb.) per box. This schedule tare includes the paper wrappers, if any, on the apples.

China clay in so-called half-ton casks. 32.6 kilograms (72 lb.) per cask.

Figs in skeleton cases. Actual tare for outer containers plus 13 percent of the gross weight of the inside wooden boxes and figs.

Fresh tomatoes. 113 grams (4 oz.) per 100 paper wrappings.

Lemons and oranges. 283 grams (10 oz.) per box and 142 grams (5 oz.) per half-box for paper wrappings, and actual tare for outer containers.

Ocher, dry, in casks. Eight percent of the gross weight; in oil in casks, 12 percent of the gross weight.

Pimentos in tins imported from Spain.

Size can	Drained weights
3 kilos	13 6 kilograms (30 lb)—case of 6 tins
794 grams (28 oz)	16 7 kilograms (36 7 lb)—case of 24 tins
425 grams (15 oz.)	8 0 kilograms (17.72 lb)—case of 24 tins
198 grams (7 oz)	3 9 kilograms (8 62 lb)—case of 24 tins
113 grams (4 oz)	2.4 kilograms (5 33 lb)—case of 24 tins

Tobacco, leaf not stemmed. 59 kilograms (13 lb.) per bale; Sumatra: actual tare for outside coverings, plus 1.9 kilograms (4 lb.) for the inside matting and, if a certificate is attached to the invoice certifying that the bales contain paper wrappings and specifying whether light or heavy paper has been used, either 113 grams (4 oz.) or 227 grams (8 oz.) for the paper wrapping according to the thickness of paper used.

For other goods dutiable on the net weight, an actual tare will be determined. An accurate tare stated on the invoice is acceptable for Customs purposes in certain circumstances.

If the importer of record files a timely application with the port director of Customs, an allowance may be made in any case for excessive moisture and impurities not usually found in or upon the particular kind of goods.

5. PACKING OF GOODS—COMMINGLING

PACKING

Information on how to pack goods for the purpose of transporting them may be obtained from shipping manuals, carriers, forwarding agents, and other sources. This chapter, therefore, deals with packing goods being exported in a way which will permit U.S. Customs officers to examine, weigh, measure, and release them promptly.

Orderly packing and proper invoicing go hand in hand. You will speed up the clearance of your goods through Customs if you:

- Invoice your goods in a systematic manner.
- Show the exact quantity of each item of goods in each box, bale, case, or other package.
- Put marks and numbers on each package.
- Show those marks or numbers on your invoice opposite the itemization of goods contained in the package that bears those marks and numbers.

When packages contain goods of one kind only, or when the goods are imported in packages the contents and values of which are uniform, the designation of packages for examination and the examination for Customs purposes are greatly facilitated. If the contents and values differ from package to package, the possibility of delay and confusion is increased. Sometimes, because of the kinds of goods or because of the unsystematic manner in which they are packed, the entire shipment must be examined.

Pack and invoice your goods in a manner which makes a speedy examination possible. Always bear in mind that it may not be possible to ascertain the contents of your packages without full examination unless your invoice clearly shows the marks and numbers on each package (whether box, case, or bale) and specifies the exact quantity of each item of adequately described goods in each marked and numbered package.

Also, be aware that Customs examines cargo for narcotics that may, unbeknownst to the shipper or the importer, be hidden inside.

This can be time-consuming and expensive for both the importer and the Customs Service. Narcotics inspections may require completely stripping a container in order to physically examine a large portion of the cargo. This labor-intensive handling of cargo, whether by Customs, labor organizations, or private individuals, results in added costs, increased delays, and possible damage to the product. Importers can expedite this inspection process by working with Customs to develop packing standards that will permit effective Customs examinations with a minimum of delay, damage, and cost.

A critical aspect in facilitating inspections is how the cargo is loaded. "Palletizing" cargo—loading it onto pallets or other consolidated units—is an effective way to expedite such examinations. Palletization allows for quick cargo removal in minutes using a forklift compared to the hours it would take manually. Another example is leaving enough space at the top of a container and an aisle down the center to allow access by a narcotic-detector dog.

Your cooperation in this respect will help Customs officers decide which packages must be opened and examined; how much weighing, counting, or measuring must be done, and whether the goods are properly marked. It will simplify the ascertainment of tare and reduce the number of samples to be taken for laboratory analysis or for other customs purposes. It will facilitate verification of the packages and contents, as well as the reporting by Customs officers of missing or excess goods. And it will minimize the possibility that the importer may be asked to resubmit for examination packages that were already released under the belief that the ones originally designated for examination were sufficient for that purpose.

It should thus be evident that packing which is in fact merely a combination or confusion of different *types* of goods makes it impracticable for Customs officers to determine the quantity of each type of product in an importation. Such packing can also lead to a variety of other complications in the entry process. No problem will arise, however, from the orderly packing of several different kinds of properly invoiced goods in a single package. It is indiscriminate packing that causes difficulty.

COMMINGLING

Except as mentioned hereafter, whenever articles subject to different rates of duty are so packed together or mingled such that Customs officers cannot readily ascertain the quantity or value of each class of articles without physical segregation of the shipment or the contents of any package thereof, the commingled articles shall be subject to the highest rate of duty applicable to any part of the commingled lot, unless the consignee or his agent segregates the merchandise under Customs supervision.

The three methods of ready ascertainment specified by General Note 17, HTSUS, are: (1) sampling, (2) verification of packing lists or other documents filed at the time of entry, or (3) evidence showing performance of commercial settlements tests generally accepted in the trade and filed in the time and manner as prescribed in the Customs Regulations.

Segregation of merchandise is at the risk and expense of the consignee. It must be done within 30 days (unless a longer time is granted) after the date of personal delivery or the date of mailing a notice to the consignee by the port director that the goods are commingled. The compensation and expenses of the Customs officers supervising the segregation must be borne by the consignee.

Assessing duty on the commingled lot at the highest applicable rate does not apply to any part of a shipment if the consignee or his agent furnishes satisfactory proof that (1) such part is commercially negligible, is not capable of segregation without excessive cost, and will not be segregated prior to its use in a manufacturing process or otherwise, and (2) the commingling was not intended to avoid the payment of lawful duties.

Any article for which such proof is furnished shall be considered for all Customs purposes as a part of the article, subject to the next lower rate of duty, with which it is commingled.

In addition, the highest-rate rule does not apply to any part of a shipment if satisfactory proof is furnished that (1) the value of the commingled articles is less than the aggregate value would be if the shipment were segregated, (2) the shipment is not capable of segregation without excessive cost and will not be segregated prior to its use in a manufacturing process or otherwise, and (3) the commingling was not intended to avoid the payment of lawful duties.

Any merchandise for which such proof is furnished shall be considered for all Customs purposes to be dutiable at the rate applicable to the material present in greater quantity than any other material.

The above rules do not apply if the tariff schedules provide a particular tariff treatment for commingled articles.

6. DEFINITION

Informed compliance is a shared responsibility between Customs and the import community wherein Customs effectively communicates its requirements to the trade, and the people and businesses subject to those requirements conduct their regulated activities in accordance with U.S. laws and regulations. A key component of informed compliance is that the importer is expected to exercise reasonable care in his or her importing operations.

Informed compliance benefits both parties: When voluntary compliance is achieved, Customs resources need not be expended on redundant examinations or entry reviews for the importer's cargo found to be dependably compliant. From the trade perspective, when voluntary compliance is attained, compliant importers are less likely to have their shipments examined or their entries reviewed.

The Customs Service publishes a wealth of information to assist the import community in complying with Customs requirements. We issue rulings and informed compliance publications on a variety of technical subjects and processes. Most of these materials can be found on-line at **www.customs.ustreas.gov**.

We urge importers to make sure they are using the latest versions of any printed materials.

7. REASONABLE CARE CHECKLISTS

Reasonable care is an explicit responsibility on the part of the importer. Despite its seemingly simple connotation, the term *reasonable care* defies easy explanation because the facts and circumstances surrounding every import transaction differ, from the experience of the importer to the nature of the imported articles. Consequently, neither the Customs Service nor the importing community can develop a reasonable care checklist capable of covering every import transaction.

The Customs Service recommends that the import community examine the list of questions below. These questions may suggest methods that importers may find useful in avoiding compliance problems and in meeting the responsibilities of reasonable care.

These questions are intended to promote compliance with Customs laws and regulations, but be aware that the list is advisory, not exhaustive. The checklist is intended as a guide and *has no legal, binding or precedential effect on Customs or the importing community.*

The questions apply whether the importer of record conducts the transactions(s) him- or herself, or whether the importer hires others to do it.

General Questions for All Transactions:

1.   If you have not retained an expert (e.g., lawyer, customs broker, accountant, or customs consultant) to assist you in complying with Customs requirements, do you have access to the *Customs Regulations* (Title 19 of the Code of Federal Regulations), the *Harmonized Tariff Schedule of the United States*, and *Customs Bulletin and Decisions*? (All three are available from the Superintendent of Documents, 202-512-1800.) Do you have access to the Customs Web site, Customs Electronic Bulletin Board, or other research service that provides the information to help you establish reliable procedures and facilitate compliance with Customs law and regulations?

2. Has a responsible, knowledgeable individual within your organization reviewed your customs documentation to assure that it is full, complete and accurate? If the documentation was prepared outside your organization, do you have a reliable method to assure that you receive copies of the information submitted to Customs, that it is reviewed for accuracy, and that Customs is apprised of needed corrections in a timely fashion?

3. If you use an expert to help you comply with Customs requirements, have you discussed your importations in advance with that person, and have you provided him or her with complete, accurate information about the import transaction(s)?

4. Are identical transactions or merchandise handled differently at different ports or Customs offices within the same port? If so, have you brought this fact to Customs officials' attention?

Questions by Topic: Merchandise Description & Tariff Classification

Basic Question: Do you know what you ordered, where it was made, and what it is made of?

1. Have you provided a complete, accurate description of your merchandise to Customs in accordance with 19 U.S.C. 1481? (Also, see 19 CFR 141.87 and 19 CFR 141.89 for special merchandise description requirements.)

2. Have you provided Customs with the correct tariff classification of your merchandise in accordance with 19 U.S.C. 1484?

3. Have you obtained a Customs ruling regarding the description of your merchandise or its tariff classification (see 19 CFR Part 177)? If so, have you followed the ruling and apprised appropriate Customs officials of those facts (i.e., of the ruling and your compliance with it)?

4. Where merchandise description or tariff classification information is not immediately available, have you established a reliable procedure for obtaining it and providing it to Customs?

5. Have you participated in a Customs pre-classification of your merchandise in order to get it properly described and classified?

6. Have you consulted the tariff schedules, Customs informed compliance publications, court cases or Customs rulings to help you properly describe and classify the merchandise?

7. Have you consulted with an expert (lawyer, customs broker, accountant, customs consultant) to assist in the description and/or classification of the merchandise?

8. If you are claiming a conditionally free or special tariff classification or provision for your merchandise (e.g., GSP, HTS Item 9802, NAFTA), how have you verified that the merchandise qualifies for such status? Do you have the documentation necessary to support the claim? If making a NAFTA preference claim, do you have a NAFTA certificate of origin in your possession?

9. Is the nature of your merchandise such that a laboratory analysis or other specialized procedure is advised for proper description and classification?

10. Have you developed reliable procedures to maintain and produce the required entry documentation and supporting information?

Valuation

Basic Questions: Do you know the "price actually paid or payable" for your merchandise? Do you know the terms of sale? Whether there will be rebates, tie-ins, indirect costs, additional payments? Whether "assists" were provided or commissions or royalties paid? Are amounts actual or estimated? Are you and the supplier "related parties"?

1. Have you provided Customs with a proper declared value for your merchandise in accordance with 19 U.S.C. 1484 and 19 U.S.C. 1401a?

2. Have you obtained a Customs ruling regarding valuation of the merchandise (see 19 CFR Part 177)? Can you establish that you followed the ruling reliably? Have you brought those facts to Customs' attention?

3. Have you consulted the Customs valuation laws and regulations, *Customs Valuation Encyclopedia*, Customs informed compliance publications, court cases and Customs rulings to assist you in valuing merchandise?

4. If you purchased the merchandise from a "related" seller, have you reported that fact upon entry? Have you assured that the value reported to Customs meets one of the "related party" tests?

5. Have you assured that all legally required costs or payments associated with the imported merchandise (assists, commissions, indirect payments or rebates, royalties, etc.) have been reported to Customs?

6. If you are declaring a value based upon a transaction in which you were/are not the buyer, have you substantiated that the transaction is a bona fide "sale at arm's length" and that the merchandise was clearly destined to the United States at the time of sale?

7. If you are claiming a conditionally free or special tariff classification or provision for your merchandise (GSP, HTS Item 9802, NAFTA), have you reported the required value information and obtained the documentation necessary to support the claim?

8. Have you produced the required entry documentation and supporting information?

Country of Origin/Marking/Quota

Basic Question: Have you ascertained the correct country of origin for the imported merchandise?

1. Have you reported the correct country of origin on Customs entry documents?

2. Have you assured that the merchandise is properly marked upon entry with the correct country of origin (if required) in accordance with 19 U.S.C. 1304 and any other applicable special marking requirements (watches, gold, textile labeling, etc)?

3. Have you obtained a Customs ruling regarding the proper marking and country of origin of the merchandise (see 19 CFR Part 177)? If so, have you followed the ruling and brought that fact to Customs attention?

4. Have you consulted with a customs expert regarding the correct country of origin/proper marking of your merchandise?

5. Have you apprised your foreign supplier of Customs country-of-origin marking requirements prior to importation of your merchandise?

6. If you are claiming a change in the origin of the merchandise or claiming that the goods are of U.S. origin, have you taken required measures to substantiate your claim (e.g., do you have U. S. milling certificates or manufacturers' affidavits attesting to production in the United States)?

7. If importing textiles or apparel, have you ascertained the correct country of origin in accordance with 19 U.S.C. 3592 (Section 334, P.L. 103-465) and assured yourself that no illegal transshipment or false or fraudulent practices were involved?

8. Do you know how your goods are made, from raw materials to finished goods, by whom and where?

9. Have you ensured that the quota category is correct?

10. Have you checked the *Status Report on Current Import Quotas* (Restraint Levels), issued by Customs, to determine if your goods are subject to a quota category with "part" categories?

11. Have you obtained correct visas for those goods subject to visa categories?

12. For textile articles, have you prepared a proper country declaration for each entry, i. e., a single country declaration (if wholly obtained/produced) or a multi-country declaration (if raw materials from one country were transformed into goods in a second)?

13. Can you produce all entry documentation and supporting information, including certificates of origin, if Customs requires you to do so?

Intellectual Property Rights

Basic Question: Have you determined whether your merchandise or its packaging use any trademarks or copyrighted material or are patented? If so, can you establish that you have a legal right to import those items into and/or use them in the United States?

1.   If you are importing goods or packaging bearing a trademark registered in the United States, have you established that it is genuine and not restricted from importation under the "gray-market" or parallel-import requirements of United States law (see 198 CFR 133.21), or that you have permission from the trademark holder to import the merchandise?

2.   If you are importing goods or packaging that contain registered copyrighted material, have you established that this material is authorized and genuine? If you are importing sound recordings of live performances, were the recordings authorized?

3.   Is your merchandise subject to an International Trade Commission or court-ordered exclusion order?

4.   Can you produce the required entry documentation and supporting information?

Miscellaneous

1.   Have you assured that your merchandise complies with other agencies' requirements (e.g., FDA, EPA, DOT, CPSC, FTC, Agriculture, etc.) and obtained licenses or permits, if required, from them?

2.   Are your goods subject to a Commerce Department dumping or countervailing-duty investigation or determination? If so, have you complied with Customs reporting requirements of this fact (e.g., 19 CFR 141.61)?

3.   Is your merchandise subject to quota/visa requirements? If so, have you provided a correct visa for the goods upon entry?

4.   Have you assured that you have the right to make entry under the Customs Regulations?

5.   Have you filed the correct type of Customs entry (e. g., TIB, T&E, consumption entry, mail entry)?

Additional Questions for Textile and Apparel Importers

Section 333 of the Uruguay Round Implementation Act (19 U. S. C. 1592a) authorizes the Secretary of the Treasury to publish a list of foreign producers, manufacturers, suppliers, sellers, exporters, or other foreign persons found to have violated 19 U.S.C. 1592 by using false, fraudulent or counterfeit documentation, labeling, or prohibited transshipment practices in connection with textiles and apparel products. Section 1592a also requires any importer of record who enters or otherwise attempts to introduce into United States commerce textile or apparel products that were directly or indirectly produced, manufactured, supplied, sold, exported, or transported by such named person(s) to show, to the Secretary's satisfaction, that the importer has exercised reasonable care to ensure that the importations are accompanied by accurate documentation, packaging and labeling regarding the products' origin. Under section 1592a, reliance solely upon information from a person named on the list does not constitute the exercise of reasonable care. Textile and apparel importers who have a commercial relationship with any of the listed parties must exercise reasonable care in ensuring that the documentation covering the imported merchandise, its packaging and its labeling accurately identify the importation's country of origin. This demonstration of reasonable care must rely upon more information than that supplied by the named party.

In order to meet the reasonable care standard when importing textile or apparel products and when dealing with a party named on this list, an importer should consider the following questions to ensure that the documentation, packaging and labeling are accurate regarding country-of-origin considerations. This list is illustrative, not exhaustive:

1.   Has the importer had a prior relationship with the named party?

2.   Has the importer had any seizures or detentions of textile or apparel products that were directly or indirectly produced, supplied, or transported by the named party?

3.   Has the importer visited the company's premises to ascertain that the company actually has the capacity to produce the merchandise?

4.   Where a claim of an origin-conferring process is made in accordance with 19 CFR 102.21, has the importer ascertained that the named party actually performed that process?

5. Is the named party really operating from the country that he or she claims on the documentation, packaging or labeling?

6. Have quotas for the imported merchandise closed, or are they near closing, from the main producer countries for this commodity?

7. Does the country have a dubious or questionable history regarding this commodity?

8. Have you questioned your supplier about the product's origin?

9. If the importation is accompanied by a visa, permit or license, has the importer verified with the supplier or manufacturer that the document is of valid, legitimate origin? Has the importer examined that document for any irregularities that would call its authenticity into question?

8. COMPLIANCE ASSESSMENT/ COMPLIANCE MEASUREMENT

Of primary interest to the trade community is the compliance assessment, which is the systematic evaluation of an importer's systems supporting his or her Customs-related operations. The assessment includes testing import and financial transactions, reviewing the adequacy of the importer's internal controls, and determining the importer's compliance levels in key areas. Compliance assessments are conducted in accordance with 19 U.S.C. 1509.

The assessment is conducted by an interdisciplinary team composed of a Customs auditor, import specialist, account manager, industry expert (highly knowledgeable of the electronics or auto parts or surgical equipment industries, for example), and possibly other Customs specialists (attorney, inspector, scientist). The compliance assessment utilizes professionally accepted statistical sampling and auditing techniques to review selected import transactions from the company's previous fiscal year.

Compliance assessments will evaluate the company's applicable customs operations such as:

■ Record keeping,

■ Merchandise classification/trade statistics,

■ Merchandise quantities,

■ Antidumping/countervailing duty operations,

■ Quota conformity,

■ Merchandise value,

■ Warehouse or foreign trade zone operations,

■ Merchandise transshipment,

■ Special trade programs (GSP, CBI, others).

Companies found in compliance with Customs laws and regulations will get a report stating that fact. Companies whose systems are determined to be noncompliant will also get a report and will be asked to formulate, in cooperation with Customs advisors, a compliance improvement plan specifying corrective actions the company will take to increase compliance levels. Serious violations of law or regulation may result in Customs referring the company for a formal investigation or other enforcement actions.

By law, Customs is required to provide the importer with advance notice of an intended assessment and an estimate of its duration. Importers are entitled to an entry conference, during which the assessment's purpose will be explained and its duration provided. Using information from Customs data bases about the company or the importer's industry, the compliance assessment team may have prepared questionnaires seeking specific information about the importer's internal procedures; these questionnaires will also be distributed at the entry conference.

Upon completion of the assessment, Customs will schedule a closing conference, at which its preliminary findings will be explained. A closing conference may not be scheduled for companies found to have serious enforcement issues. If no enforcement action is taken, Customs will provide the company with a written report of the assessment's results.

The Importer Audit/Compliance Assessment Team Kit (also called the CAT Kit), which provides extensive details of the assessment procedure, can be found at Customs' Web site, **www.customs.ustreas.gov**, or by calling the Customs Regulatory Audit Division office nearest you.

Compliance Measurement is the primary tool Customs uses to assess the accuracy of port-of-entry transactions and to determine the compliance rate for all commercial importations. By using statistical sampling methods, a valid compliance level for all commercial importations can be obtained. One of the Customs Service's goals is to assure that at least 99 percent of the import revenues legally owed the United States government are collected. Cargo is sampled for compliance with international trade laws at the port of entry, at the time of entry into the United States. Importers should be aware that misclassification of merchandise, among other violations, will be detected through the compliance measurement process.

9. A NOTICE TO SMALL-BUSINESS IMPORTERS

The Small Business Regulatory Enforcement Fairness Act was designed to create a more cooperative regulatory environment between federal agencies and small businesses.

Your comments are important. The Small Business and Regulatory Enforcement Ombudsman and 10 regional Fairness Boards were established to receive comments from small businesses about federal agency enforcement activities and to rate each agency's responsiveness to small business. If you wish to comment on the enforcement actions of the U.S. Customs Service, call 1-888-REG-FAIR (1-888-734-3247).

10. COMMERCIAL INVOICE

A commercial invoice, signed by the seller or shipper, or his agent, is acceptable for customs purposes if it is prepared in accordance with Section 141.86 through 141.89 of the Customs Regulations, and in the manner customary for a commercial transaction involving goods of the kind covered by the invoice. Importers and brokers participating in the Automated Broker Interface may elect to transmit invoice data via the Automated Invoice Interface or EDIFACT and eliminate the paper document. The invoice must provide the following information, as required by the Tariff Act:

■ The port of entry to which the merchandise is destined;

■ If merchandise is sold or agreed to be sold, the time, place, and names of buyer and seller; if consigned, the time and origin of shipment, and names of shipper and receiver;

■ A detailed description of the merchandise, including the name by which each item is known, the grade or quality, and the marks, numbers, and symbols under which sold by the seller or manufacturer to the trade in the country of exportation, together with the marks and numbers of the packages in which the merchandise is packed;

■ The quantities in weights and measures;

■ If sold or agreed to be sold, the purchase price of each item in the currency of the sale;

■ If the merchandise is shipped for consignment, the value of each item in the currency in which the transactions are usually made, or, in the absence of such value, the price in such currency that the manufacturer, seller, shipper, or owner would have received, or was willing to receive, for such merchandise if sold in the ordinary course of trade and in the usual wholesale quantities in the country of exportation;

■ The kind of currency;

■ All charges upon the merchandise, itemized by name and amount including freight, insurance, commission, cases, containers, coverings, and cost of packing; and, if not included above, all charges, costs, and expenses incurred in bringing the merchandise from alongside the carrier at the port of exportation in the country of exportation and placing it alongside the carrier at the first U.S. port of entry. The cost of packing, cases, containers, and inland freight to the port of exportation need not be itemized by amount if included in the invoice price and so identified. Where the required information does not appear on the invoice as originally prepared, it shall be shown on an attachment to the invoice;

■ All rebates, drawbacks, and bounties, separately itemized, allowed upon the exportation of the merchandise;

■ The country of origin; and

■ All goods or services furnished for the production of the merchandise not included in the invoice price.

If the merchandise on the documents is sold while in transit, the original invoice reflecting this transaction and the resale invoice or a statement of sale showing the price paid for each item by the purchaser shall be filed as part of the entry, entry summary, or withdrawal documentation.

The invoice and all attachments must be in the English language, or shall be accompanied by an accurate English translation.

Each invoice shall state in adequate detail what merchandise is contained in each individual package.

If the invoice or entry does not disclose the weight, gauge, or measure of the merchandise necessary to ascertain duties, the importer of record shall pay expenses incurred to obtain this information prior to the release of the merchandise from Customs custody.

Each invoice shall set forth in detail, for each class or kind of merchandise, every discount from list or other base price which has been or may be allowed in fixing each purchaser price or value.

When more than one invoice is included in the same entry, each invoice with its attachments shall be numbered consecutively by the importer on the bottom of the face of each page, beginning with number 1. If an invoice is more than two pages, begin with number 1 for the first page of the first invoice and continue in a single series of numbers through all the invoices and attachments included in one entry. If an entry covers one invoice of one page and a second invoice of two pages, the numbering at the bottom of the page shall be as follows: Inv. 1, p.1; Inv. 2, p.2; Inv. 2, p.3, etc.

Any information required on an invoice may be set forth either on the invoice or on the attachment.

SPECIFIC REQUIREMENTS

1. Separate Invoice Required for Each Shipment. Not more than one distinct shipment from one consignor to one consignee by one commercial carrier shall be included on the same invoice.

2. Assembled Shipments. Merchandise assembled for shipment to the same consignee by one commercial carrier may be included in one invoice. The original bills or invoices covering the merchandise, or extracts therefrom, showing the actual price paid or agreed to be paid, should be attached to the invoice.

3. Installment Shipments. Installments of a shipment covered by a single order or contract and shipped from one consignor to one consignee may be included in one invoice if the installments arrive at the port of entry by any means of transportation within a period not to exceed 10 consecutive days.

The invoice should be prepared in the same manner as invoices covering single shipments and should include any additional information which may be required for the particular class of goods concerned. If it is practical to do so, the invoice should show the quantities, values, and other invoice data with respect to each installment, and the identification of the importing conveyance in which each installment was shipped.

4. Production "Assist." The invoice should indicate whether the production of merchandise involved costs for "assists" (i.e., dies, molds, tooling, printing plates, artwork, engineering work, design and development, financial assistance, etc.) which are not included in the invoice price. If assists were involved, state their value, if known, and by whom supplied. Were they supplied without cost, or on a rental basis, or were they invoiced separately? If the latter, attach a copy of the invoice.

Whenever U.S. Customs requires information on the cost of production of goods for customs valuation, the importer will be notified by the port director. Thereafter, invoices covering shipments of such goods must contain a statement on the cost of production by the manufacturer or producer.

5. Additional Information Required. Special information may be required on certain goods or classes of goods in addition to the information normally required on the invoice. Although the United States importer usually advises the exporter of these special situations, section 141.89 of the Customs Regulations, which covers the requirements for these goods, has been reproduced in the appendix.

6. Rates of Exchange. In general, no rate(s) of exchange may be used to convert foreign currency for customs purposes other than the rate(s) proclaimed or certified in 31 U.S.C. 5151. For merchandise imported from a country having a currency for which two or more rates of exchange have been certified by the Federal Reserve Bank of New York, the invoice will show the exchange rate or rates used in converting the United States dollars received for the merchandise into the foreign currency and the percentage of each rate if two or more rates are used. If a rate or combination of rates used to pay costs, charges, or expenses is different from those used to pay for the merchandise, state that rate or combination of rates separately. Where dollars have not been converted at the time the invoice is prepared, state that fact on the invoice, in which case the invoice shall also state the rate or combination of rates at which the dollars will be converted, or that it is not known what rate or rates will be used. Rates of exchange are not required for merchandise unconditionally free of duty or subject only to a specific rate of duty not depending on value.

11. OTHER INVOICES

PRO FORMA INVOICE

If the required commercial invoice is not filed at the time the merchandise is entered, a statement in the form of an invoice (a *pro forma* invoice) must be filed by the importer at the time of entry. A bond is given for production of the required invoice not later than 120 days from the date of the entry summary, or entry if there is no entry summary. If the invoice is needed for statistical purposes, it must generally be produced within 50 days from the date on which the entry summary is required to be filed.

The exporter should bear in mind that unless he or she forwards the required invoice in time, the American importer will incur a liability under his bond for failure to file the invoice with the port director of Customs before the 120-day period expires.

Although a pro forma invoice is not prepared by the exporter, it is of interest to exporters as it gives a general idea of the kind of information needed for entry purposes. A pro forma invoice indicates what the importer may find necessary to furnish Customs officers at the time a formal entry is filed for a commercial shipment if a properly prepared customs or commercial invoice is not available at the time the goods are entered. An acceptable format for a pro forma invoice is reproduced in the appendix.

Some of the additional information specified for the commodities under section 141.89 of the Customs Regulations may not be required when entry is made on a pro forma invoice. However, the pro forma invoice must contain sufficient data for examination, classification, and appraisement purposes.

SPECIAL INVOICES

Special invoices are required for some merchandise. See 19 CFR 141.89.

12. FREQUENT ERRORS IN INVOICING

Foreign sellers or shippers must exercise care in preparing invoices and other documents used to enter goods into the commerce of the United States in order for their importers to avoid difficulties, delays, or possibly even penal sanctions. Each document must contain all information required by law or regulations, and every statement of fact contained in the documents must be true and accurate. Any inaccurate or misleading statement of fact in a document presented to a Customs officer in connection with an entry, or the omission from the document of required information, may result in delays in merchandise release, the detention of the goods, or a claim against the importer for domestic value. Even though the inaccuracy or omission was unintentional, the importer may be required to establish that he exercised due diligence and was not negligent, in order to avoid sanctions with consequent delay in obtaining possession of goods and closing the transaction. (See 19 U.S.C. 1592.)

It is particularly important that all statements relating to merchandise description, price or value, and amounts of discounts, charges, and commissions be truthfully and accurately set forth. It is also important that the invoices set forth the true name of the actual seller and purchaser of the goods, in the case of purchased goods, or the true name of the actual consignor and consignee when the goods are shipped otherwise than in pursuance of a purchase. It is important, too, that the invoice otherwise reflect the real nature of the transaction pursuant to which the goods were shipped to the United States.

The fundamental rule is that both the shipper and importer must furnish Customs officers with all pertinent information with respect to each import transaction to assist Customs officers in determining the tariff status of the goods. Examples of omissions and inaccuracies to be avoided are:

- The shipper assumes that a commission, royalty, or other charge against the goods is a so-called "nondutiable" item and omits it from the invoice.

- A foreign shipper who purchases goods and sells them to a United States importer at a delivered price shows on the invoice the cost of the goods to him instead of the delivered price.

- A foreign shipper manufactures goods partly with the use of materials supplied by the United States importer, but invoices the goods at the actual cost to the manufacturer without including the value of the materials supplied by the importer.

- The foreign manufacturer ships replacement goods to his customer in the United States and invoices the goods at the net price without showing the full price less the allowance for defective goods previously shipped and returned.

- A foreign shipper who sells goods at list price, less a discount, invoices them at the net price, and fails to show the discount.

- A foreign shipper sells goods at a delivered price but invoices them at a price f.o.b. the place of shipment and omits the subsequent charges.

- A foreign shipper indicates in the invoice that the importer is the purchaser, whereas he is in fact either an agent who is receiving a commission for selling the goods or a party who will receive part of the proceeds of the sale of the goods sold for the joint account of the shipper and consignee.

- Invoice descriptions are vague, listing only parts of numbers, truncated or coded descriptions, or lumping various articles together as one when several distinct items are included.

13. DUTIABLE STATUS OF GOODS

RATES OF DUTY

All goods imported into the United States are subject to duty or duty-free entry in accordance with their classification under the applicable items in the Harmonized Tariff Schedule of the United States. An annotated looseleaf edition of the tariff schedule may be purchased from the U.S. Government Printing Office, Washington, DC 20402. (See 19 U.S.C. 1202.)

When goods are dutiable, *ad valorem*, specific, or compound rates may be assessed. An ad valorem rate, which is the type of rate most often applied, is a percentage of value of the merchandise, such as five percent ad valorem. A specific rate is a specified amount per unit of weight or other quantity, such as 5.9 cents per dozen. A compound rate is a combination of both an ad valorem rate and a specific rate, such as 0.7 cents per kilo plus 10 percent ad valorem.

FREE OF DUTY OR DUTIABLE

Rates of duty for imported merchandise may also vary depending upon the country of origin. Most merchandise is dutiable under the most-favored-nation—now referred to as *normal trade relations*—rates in the General column under column 1 of the tariff schedule. Merchandise from countries to which these rates have *not* been extended is dutiable at the full or "statutory" rates in column 2 of the tariff schedule.

Free rates are provided for many subheadings in columns 1 and 2 of the tariff schedule. Duty-free status is also available under various conditional exemptions which are reflected in the Special column under column 1 of the tariff schedule. It is the importer's burden to show eligibility for a conditional exemption from duty.

One of the more frequently applied exemptions from duty occurs under the General-

ized System of Preferences (GSP). GSP-eligible merchandise qualifies for duty-free entry when it is from a beneficiary developing country and meets other requirements as discussed in Chapter 17. Other exemptions are found under the subheadings in Chapter 98 of the tariff schedule. These subheadings include, among other provisions, certain personal exemptions, exemptions for articles for scientific or other institutional purposes, and exemptions for returned American goods.

RULINGS ON IMPORTS

The Customs Service makes its decision on the dutiable status of merchandise when the entry is liquidated after the entry documents have been filed. When advance information is needed, do not depend on a small "trial" or "test" shipment since there is no guarantee that the next shipment will receive the same tariff treatment. Small importations may slip by, particularly if they are processed under informal procedures that apply to small shipments or in circumstances warranting application of a flat rate. An exporter, importer, or other interested party may get advance information on any matter affecting the dutiable status of merchandise by writing to the port director where the merchandise will be entered or to the National Commodity Specialist Division, New York, NY 10048, or to the U.S. Customs Service, Attention: Office of Regulations and Rulings, Washington, DC 20229. Detailed information on the procedures applicable to decisions on prospective importations is given in 19 CFR Part 177.

BINDING DECISIONS

While you will find that, for many purposes, Customs ports are your best sources of information, informal information obtained on tariff classifications is not binding. Under 19 CFR part 177, the importing public may obtain a binding tariff classification ruling, which can be relied upon for placing or accepting orders or for making other business determinations, under Chapters 1 through 97 of the Harmonized Tariff Schedule, by writing to any Customs port director or to the National Commodity Specialist Division, 6 World Trade Center, New York, NY 10048. The ruling will be binding at all ports of entry unless revoked by the Customs Service's Office of Regulations and Rulings.

The following information is required in ruling requests:

■ The names, addresses and other identifying information of all interested parties (if known) and the manufacturer ID code (if known).

■ The name(s) of the port(s) at which the merchandise will be entered (if known).

■ A description of the transaction; for example, a prospective importation of (merchandise) from (country).

■ A statement that there are, to the importer's knowledge, no issues on the commodity pending before the Customs Service or any court.

■ A statement as to whether classification advice has previously been sought from a Customs officer, and if so, from whom, and what advice was rendered, if any.

A request for a tariff classification should include the following information:

■ A complete description of the goods. Send samples, if practical, sketches, diagrams, or other illustrative material that will be useful in supplementing the written description.

■ Cost breakdowns of component materials and their respective quantities shown in percentages, if possible.

■ A description of the principal use of the goods, as a class or kind of merchandise, in the United States.

■ Information as to commercial, scientific or common designations, as may be applicable.

■ Any other information that may be pertinent or required for the purpose of tariff classification.

Any of the first four requirements above may be disregarded if you are certain the information will not be of use for tariff classification purposes. However, to avoid delays, your request should be as complete as possible. If you send a sample, do not rely on it to tell the whole story. Also, please note that samples may be subjected to laboratory analysis, which is done free of charge. Clearly, however, if a sample is destroyed during laboratory analysis, it cannot be returned.

Information submitted and incorporated in response to a request for a Customs decision may be disclosed or withheld in accordance with the provisions of the Freedom of Information Act, as amended 5 U.S.C. 552, 19 CFR 177.8(a)(3)).

PROTESTS

The importer may disagree with the dutiable status after the entry has been liquidated. A decision at this stage of the entry transaction is requested by filing a protest and application for further review on Customs Form 19 within 90 days after liquidation (see CFR part 174). If the Customs Service denies a protest, dutiable status may then be determined through litigation against the Government.

LIABILITY FOR DUTIES

There is no provision under which U.S. duties or taxes may be prepaid in a foreign country before exportation to the United States. This is true even for gifts sent by mail.

In the usual case, liability for the payment of duty becomes fixed at the time an entry for consumption or for warehouse is filed with Customs. The obligation for payment is upon the person or firm in whose name the entry is filed. When goods have been entered for warehouse, liability for paying duties may be transferred to any person who purchases the goods and desires to withdraw them in his or her own name.

Paying a customs broker will not relieve the importer of his or her liability for customs charges (duties, taxes, and other debts owed Customs) should those charges not be paid by the broker. Therefore, if the importer pays the broker by check, he should give the broker a separate check, made payable to "U.S. Customs Service" for those customs charges, which the broker will then deliver to Customs.

If the entry is made in the name of a customs broker, the broker may obtain relief from statutory liability for the payment of increased or additional duties found due if (1) the actual owner of goods is named, and (2) the owner's declaration whereby the owner agrees to pay the additional duty and the owner's bond are both filed by the broker with the port director within 90 days of the date of entry.

14. CONTAINERS OR HOLDERS

The Customs Service designates such items as lift vans, cargo vans, shipping tanks, pallets and certain articles used to ship goods internationally as *instruments of international traffic*. So long as this designation applies, these articles are not subject to entry or duty when they arrive, whether they are loaded or empty. Other classes of merchandise containers may also be designated as *instruments of international traffic* upon application to the Commissioner of Customs for such a designation. If any article so designated is diverted to domestic use, however, it must be entered and duty paid, if applicable.

Containers specially shaped or fitted to contain a specific article or set of articles, suitable for long term use and entered with the articles for which they are intended, are classifiable with the accompanying articles if they are of a kind normally sold therewith. Examples of such containers are: camera cases, musical instrument cases, gun cases, drawing instrument cases, and necklace cases. This rule does not apply to containers that give the importation as a whole its essential character.

Subject to the above rule, packing materials and packing containers entered with goods packed in them are classified with these goods if they are of a kind normally used for packing such goods. However, this does not apply to packing materials or containers that are clearly suitable for repetitive use.

15. TEMPORARY FREE IMPORTATIONS

TEMPORARY IMPORTATION UNDER BOND (TIB)

Goods of the types enumerated below, when not imported for sale or for sale on approval, may be admitted into the United States under bond, without the payment of duty, for exportation within one year from the date of importation. Generally, the amount of the bond is double the estimated duties. The one-year period for exportation may, upon application to the port director, be extended for one or more further periods which, when added to the initial one year, shall not exceed a total of three years. There is an exception in the case of articles covered in item 14: the period of the bond may not exceed six months and may not be extended.

Merchandise entered under TIB must be exported before expiration of the bond period, or any extension, to avoid assessment of liquidated damages in the amount of the bond.

All goods entered under TIB are subject to quota compliance.

CLASSES OF GOODS

(1)   Merchandise to be repaired, altered, or processed (including processes which result in an article being manufactured or produced in the United States), provided that the following conditions are met:

- The merchandise will not be processed into an article manufactured or produced in the United States if the article is (1) alcohol, distilled spirits, wine, beer, or any dilution or mixture of these; (2) perfume or other commodity containing ethyl alcohol, whether denatured or not; (3) a product of wheat.

- If merchandise is processed and results in an article being manufactured or produced in the United States other than those described above, (1) a complete accounting will be made to the Customs Service for all articles, wastes, and irrecoverable losses resulting from the processing, and (2) all articles will be exported or destroyed under Customs supervision within the bonded period. Valuable waste must also be exported or so destroyed unless duty, if applicable, is paid.

(2)   Models of women's wearing apparel imported by manufacturers for use solely as models in their own establishments; these articles require quota compliance.

(3)   Articles imported by illustrators and photographers for use solely as models in their own establishments to illustrate catalogs, pamphlets, or advertising matter.

(4)   Samples solely for use in taking orders for merchandise; these samples require quota compliance.

(5)   Articles solely for examination with a view to reproduction or for examination and reproduction (except photoengraved printing plates for examination and reproduction); and motion-picture advertising films.

(6)   Articles intended solely for testing, experimental, or review purposes, including plans, specifications, drawings, blueprints, photographs, and articles for use in connection with experiments or for study. If articles under this category are destroyed in connection with the experiment or study, proof of such destruction must be presented to satisfy the obligation under the bond to export the articles.

(7)   Automobiles, motorcycles, bicycles, airplanes, airships, balloons, boats, racing shells, and similar vehicles and craft, and the usual equipment of the foregoing, if brought temporarily into the United States by nonresidents for the purpose of taking part in races or other specific contests. Port directors may defer the exaction of a bond for a period not to exceed 90 days after the date of importation for vehicles and craft to take part in races or other specific contests for other than money purposes. If the vehicle or craft is not exported or the bond is not given within the period of such deferment, the vehicle or craft shall be subject to forfeiture.

(8)   Locomotives and other railroad equipment brought temporarily into the United States for use in clearing obstructions, fighting fires, or making emergency repairs on railroads within the United States or for use in transportation otherwise than in international traffic when the Secretary of the Treasury finds that the temporary use of foreign railroad equipment is necessary to meet an emergency. Importers can expedite approval of a request for temporary importation to meet an emergency by including evidence of the existence of the emergency, such as news reports.

(9)   Containers for compressed gases, filled or empty, and containers or other articles used for covering or holding merchandise (including personal or household effects) during transportation and suitable for reuse for that purpose.

(10) Professional equipment, tools of trade, repair components for equipment or tools admitted under this item, and camping equipment imported by or for nonresidents for the nonresident's use while sojourning temporarily in the United States.

(11) Articles of special design for temporary use exclusively in connection with the manufacture or production of articles for export.

(12) Animals and poultry brought into the United States for the purpose of breeding, exhi-

bition, or competition for prizes, and the usual equipment therefor.

(13) Works of free fine arts, drawings, engravings, photographic pictures, and philosophical and scientific apparatus brought into the United States by professional artists, lecturers, or scientists arriving from abroad for use by them for exhibition and in illustration, promotion, and encouragement of art, science or industry in the United States.

(14) Automobiles, automobile chassis, automobile bodies, cutaway portions of any of the foregoing, and parts for any of the foregoing, finished, unfinished, or cutaway, when intended solely for show purposes. These articles may be admitted only on condition that the Secretary of the Treasury has found that the foreign country from which the articles were imported allows or will allow substantially reciprocal privileges with respect to similar exports to that country from the United States. If the Secretary finds that a foreign country has discontinued or will discontinue the allowance of such privileges, the privileges under this item shall not apply thereafter to imports from that country.

RELIEF FROM LIABILITY

Relief from liability under bond may be obtained in any case in which the articles are destroyed under Customs supervision, in lieu of exportation, within the original bond period. However, in the case of articles entered under item 6, destruction need not be under Customs supervision where articles are destroyed during the course of experiments or tests during the bond period or any lawful extension, but satisfactory proof of destruction shall be furnished to the port director with whom the customs entry is filed.

ATA CARNET

ATA stands for the combined French and English words "Admission Temporaire—Temporary Admission." ATA carnet is an international customs document which may be used for the temporary duty-free importation of certain goods into a country in lieu of the usual customs documents required. The carnet serves as a guarantee against the payment of customs duties which may become due on goods temporarily imported and not reexported. Quota compliance is required on merchandise subject to quota; for example, textiles are subject to quota and visa requirements.

A carnet is valid for one year. The traveler or businessperson, however, may make as many trips as desired during the period the carnet is valid provided he or she has sufficient pages for each stop.

The United States currently allows ATA carnets to be used for the temporary admission of professional equipment, commercial samples, and advertising material. Most other countries allow the use of carnets for the temporary admission of these goods and, in some cases, other uses of the ATA carnet are permitted.

Local carnet associations, as members of the International Bureau of the Paris-based International Chamber of Commerce, issue carnets to their residents. These associations guarantee the payment of duties to local customs authorities should goods imported under cover of a foreign-issued carnet not be reexported. In the United States, the U.S. Council of the International Chamber of Commerce, located at 1212 Avenue of the Americas, New York, NY 10036, (212) 354-4480, has been designated by U.S. Customs as the United States issuing and guaranteeing organization. A fee is charged by the Council for its service.

ATA carnets can be used in the following countries:

Algeria	France	Japan	Singapore
Australia	French Polynesia	Republic of South Korea	Slovakia
Austria	French West Indies	Lebanon	Slovenia
Belgium	Germany	Luxembourg	South Africa
Bulgaria	Gibraltar	Malaysia	Spain
Canada	Greece	Malta	Sri Lanka
Canary Islands	Hong Kong	Mauritius	Sweden
China	Hungary	Netherlands	Switzerland
Croatia	Iceland	New Zealand	Thailand
Cyprus	India	Norway	Turkey
Czech Republic	Ireland	Poland	United Kingdom
Denmark	Israel	Portugal	United States
Estonia	Italy	Romania	
Finland	Ivory Coast	Senegal	

Egypt and certain other countries have accepted the ATA convention but have not implemented the use of carnets. As countries are being continuously added to the carnet system, please check with the U.S. Council if a country you wish to visit is not included in the above list.

16. THE NORTH AMERICAN FREE TRADE AGREEMENT (NAFTA)

The provisions of the North American Free Trade Agreement were adopted by the United States with enactment of the North American Free Trade Agreement Implementation Act of 1993 (107 Stat. 2057, Public Law 103-182). Nineteen CFR Parts 10, 12, 123, 134, 162, 174, 177, 178 were amended and new parts 102 and 181 of the Customs Regulations were developed to implement the duty provisions of the NAFTA.

The NAFTA eliminates tariffs on most goods originating in Canada, Mexico, and the United States over a maximum transition period of fifteen years. The schedule to eliminate tariffs already established in the Canada-United States Free Trade Agreement will continue as planned so that all Canada-United States trade will be duty-free in 1998. For most Mexico-United States and Canada-Mexico trade, the NAFTA will either eliminate existing customs duties immediately or phase them out in five to ten years. On a few sensitive items, the Agreement will phase out tariffs over fifteen years. NAFTA-member countries may agree to a faster phase-out of tariffs on any goods.

During the transition period, rates of duties will vary depending upon which NAFTA country the goods were produced in. That is, the NAFTA may grant Canadian goods entering the United States a different NAFTA rate than the same Mexican goods entering the United States. For most goods imported into Canada, there will be three NAFTA rates; the rate depends on whether the goods are of U.S. origin, Mexican origin or produced jointly with U.S. and Mexican inputs.

Generally, tariffs will only be eliminated on goods that "originate" as defined in Article 401 of the NAFTA. That is, transshipping goods made in another country through Mexico or Canada will not entitle them to preferential NAFTA rates of duty. The NAFTA does provide for reduced duties on some goods of Canada, Mexico, and the United States that do not originate there but that meet specified conditions outlined in the Agreement. The NAFTA grants benefits to a variety of goods that "originate" in the region. "Originating" is a term used to describe those goods that meet the requirements of Article 401 of the Agreement. Article 401 of the Agreement defines "originating" in four ways:

■ Goods wholly obtained or produced entirely in the NAFTA region;

- Goods produced entirely in the NAFTA region exclusively from originating materials;
- Goods meeting a specific Annex 401 origin rule;
- Unassembled goods and goods classified with their parts which do not meet the Annex 401 rule of origin but contain 60 percent regional value content using the transaction method (50 percent using the net cost method.)

Goods that qualify as originating will lose that status if they subsequently undergo any operation outside the NAFTA region other than unloading, reloading, or any other operation necessary to preserve them in good condition or to transport the goods to Canada, Mexico or the United States.

ENTRY PROCEDURES

Existing entry procedures will continue to be used under the NAFTA. As with other trade-preference programs, importers must claim NAFTA benefits to receive preferential duty treatment. In the United States, a claim is made by:

FORMAL ENTRIES

- Prefixing "MX" or "CA" to the tariff classification number.
- Signing the CF 7501 (Entry Summary).

INFORMAL ENTRIES

Pursuant to 19 CFR 181.22(d) of the Agreement, the U.S. does not require a Certificate of Origin for entries valued at US $2500 or less. For commercial shipments, however, the invoice accompanying the importation must include a statement certifying that the goods qualify as originating goods.

EXPORTER'S CERTIFICATE OF ORIGIN

Article 502 of the NAFTA requires that an importer base his claims on the exporter's written certificate of origin. This may be the U.S.-approved CF 434, CERTIFICATE OF ORIGIN; the Canadian Certificate of Origin (Canadian Form B-232), or the Mexican Certificate of Origin (Certificado de Origen). This certificate may cover a single shipment or may be utilized as a blanket declaration for a period of 12 months. In either case, the certificate must be in the importer's possession when making the claim.

SPECIAL PROVISIONS FOR SENSITIVE SECTORS

NAFTA Annex 401, origin criteria for textiles and apparel products, ensures that most of the production relating to textiles and apparel occurs in North America. The basic origin rule for textiles and apparel is "yarn forward." This means that the yarn used to form the fabric must originate in a NAFTA country.

Additional information on NAFTA provisions is contained in the book "The North American Free Trade Agreement: *A Guide To Customs Procedures,*" Customs Publication No. 571. This publication may be purchased from the U.S. Government Printing Office.

17. GENERALIZED SYSTEM OF PREFERENCES (GSP)

The Generalized System of Preferences (GSP) is a program providing for free rates of duty for certain merchandise from beneficiary developing independent countries and dependent countries and territories to encourage their economic growth (see below). This program was enacted by the United States in the Trade Act of 1974. It expires on June 30, 1999. Notification to the trade community will be published should the program be renewed by Congress.

ELIGIBLE ITEMS

The GSP eligibility list contains a wide range of products classifiable under more than 4,000 different subheadings in the Harmonized Tariff Schedule of the United States. These items are identified either by an "A" or "A*" in the "Special" column under column 1 of the tariff schedule. Merchandise classifiable under a subheading designated in this manner may qualify for duty-free entry if imported into the United States directly from any of the designated countries and territories. Merchandise from one or more of these countries, however, may be excluded from the exemption if there is an "A*" in the "Special" column. The list of countries and exclusions, as well as the list of GSP-eligible articles, will change from time to time over the life of the program. Therefore, the latest edition of the Harmonized Tariff Schedule of the United States will contain the most current information.

If advance tariff classification information is needed to ascertain whether your commodity is eligible under the GSP, you may obtain this information under the procedures previously discussed in Chapter 13 relating to dutiable status.

CLAIMS

For commercial shipments requiring a formal entry, a claim for duty-free status is made under GSP by showing on the entry summary that the country of origin is a designated beneficiary developing country and by showing an "A" with the appropriate GSP-eligible subheading. Eligible merchandise will be entitled to duty-free treatment provided the following conditions are met:

- The merchandise must have been produced in a beneficiary country. This requirement is satisfied when (1) the goods are wholly the growth, product, or manufacture of a beneficiary country, or (2) the goods have been substantially transformed into a new or different article of commerce in a beneficiary country.

- The merchandise must be imported directly from any beneficiary country into the customs territory of the United States.

- The cost or value of materials produced in the beneficiary developing country and/or the direct cost of processing performed there must represent at least 35 percent of the appraised value of the goods.

The cost or value of materials imported into the beneficiary developing country may be included in calculating the 35 percent value-added requirement for an eligible article if the materials are first substantially transformed into new or different articles and are then used as constituent materials in the production of the eligible article. The phrase "direct costs of processing" includes costs directly incurred or reasonably allocated to the processing of the article such as the cost of all actual labor, dies, molds, tooling, depreciation on machinery, research and development, and inspection and testing. Business overhead, administrative expenses, salaries, and profit, as well as general business expenses such as administrative salaries, casualty and liability insurance, advertising and salesmen's salaries, are not considered direct costs of processing.

SOURCES OF ADDITIONAL INFORMATION

Customs rules and regulations on GSP are incorporated in sections 10.171-10.178 of the Customs Regulations. Address any question you may have on the administrative or operational aspects of the GSP to the Director, Trade Compliance Division, U.S. Customs Service, Washington, DC 20229. Requests for information concerning additions to, or deletions from, the list of eligible merchandise under GSP, or the list of beneficiary development countries, should be directed to the Chairman, Trade Policy Staff Subcommittee, Office of U.S. Trade Representative, 600 17th St., NW, Washington, DC 20506.

GENERALIZED SYSTEM OF PREFERENCES (GSP)
Independent Countries

Albania	Czech Republic	Lithuania	Senegal
Angola	Djibouti	Macedonia,	Seychelles
Antigua and Barbuda***	Dominica***	Former Yugolslav Republic of	Sierra Leone
Argentina	Dominican Republic	Madagascar	Slovakia
Armenia	Ecuador*	Malawi	Slovenia
Bahamas***	Egypt	Malaysia**	Solomon Islands
Bahrain	El Salvador	Mali	Somalia
Bangladesh	Equatorial Guinea	Malta	South Africa
Barbados***	Estonia	Mauritius	Sri Lanka
Belarus	Ethiopia	Moldova	Surinam
Belize***	Fiji	Montserrat**	Swaziland
Benin	Gambia, The	Morocco	Tanzania
Bhutan	Ghana	Mozambique	Thailand**
Bolivia*	Grenada***	Namibia	Togo
Bosnia and Hercegovina	Guatemala	Nepal	Tonga
Botswana	Guinea	Niger	Trinidad and Tobago***
Brazil	Guinea Bissau	Oman	Tunisia
Bulgaria	Guyana***	Pakistan	Turkey
Burkina Faso	Haiti	Panama	Tuvalu
Burundi	Honduras	Papua, New Guinea	Uganda
Cambodia	Hungary	Paraguay	Ukraine
Cameroon	India	Peru*	Uruguay
Cape Verde	Indonesia**	Philippines**	Uzbekistan
Central African Republic	Jamaica***	Poland	Vanuatu
Chad	Jordan	Romania	Venezuela*
Chile	Kazakhstan	Russia	Western Samoa
Colombia*	Kenya	Rwanda	Yemen Arab Republic (Sanaa)
Comoros	Kiribati	Saint Kitts and Nevis***	Zaire
Congo	Kyrgyzstan	Saint Lucia***	Zambia
Costa Rica	Latvia	Saint Vincent and	Zimbabwe
Côte d'Ivoire	Lebanon	the Grenadines***	
Croatia	Lesotho	Sao Tome and Principe	

NON-INDEPENDENT COUNTRIES AND TERRITORIES

Anguilla	(Islas Malvinas)	Niue	Virgin Islands, British
British Indian	French Polynesia	Norfolk Island	Wallis and Funtuna
Ocean Territory	Gibraltar	Pitcairn Island	West Bank and Gaza Strip
Christmas Island (Australia)	Heard Island and	Saint Helena	Western Sahara
Cocos (Keeling) Island	McDonald Islands	Tokelau	
Cook Islands	Montserrat***	Turks and	
Falkland Islands	New Caledonia	Caicos Islands	

* Member countries of the Cartagena Agreement—Andean Group (treated as one country)
** Association of South East Asian Nations—ASEAN (GSP-eligible countries only) treated as one country.
*** Member countries of the Caribbean Common Market—CARICOM (treated as one country)

18. CARIBBEAN BASIN INITIATIVE (CBI)

The Caribbean Basin Initiative (CBI) is a program providing for the duty-free entry of certain merchandise from designated beneficiary countries or territories. This program was enacted by the United States as the Caribbean Basin Economic Recovery Act, became effective on January 1, 1984, and has no expiration date.

BENEFICIARY COUNTRIES

The following countries and territories have been designated as beneficiary countries for purposes of the CBI:

Antigua and Barbuda	Dominican Republic	Jamaica	Saint Vincent and the
Aruba	El Salvador	Montserrat	Grenadines
Bahamas	Grenada	Netherlands Antilles	Trinidad and Tobago
Barbados	Guatemala	Nicaragua	Virgin Islands,
Belize	Guyana	Panama	British
Costa Rica	Haiti	Saint Kitts and Nevis	
Dominica	Honduras	Saint Lucia	

ELIGIBLE ITEMS

The list of beneficiaries may change from time to time over the life of the program. Therefore, it is necessary to consult General Note 7(a) in the latest edition of the Harmonized Tariff Schedule of the United States, which contains updated information.

Most products from designated beneficiaries may be eligible for CBI duty-free treatment. These items are identified by either an "E" or "E*" in the Special column under column 1 of the Harmonized Tariff Schedule. Merchandise classifiable under a subheading designated in this manner may qualify for duty-free entry if imported into the United States directly from any of the designated countries and territories. Merchandise from one or more of these countries, however, may be excluded from time to time over the life of the program. Therefore, the latest edition of the Harmonized Tariff Schedule of the United States will contain the most up-to-date information.

CLAIMS

Merchandise will be eligible for CBI duty-free treatment only if the following conditions are met:

- For commercial shipments requiring a formal entry, a claim for preferential tariff treatment under CBI is made by showing that the country of origin is a designated beneficiary country and by inserting the letter "E" as a prefix to the applicable tariff schedule number on Customs Form 7501.

- The merchandise must have been produced in a beneficiary country. This requirement is satisfied when (1) the goods are wholly the growth, product, or manufacture of a beneficiary country, or (2) the goods have been substantially transformed into a new or different article of commerce in a beneficiary country.

- The merchandise must be imported directly from any beneficiary country into the customs territory of the United States.

- At least 35 percent of the appraised value of the article imported into the United States must consist of the cost or value of materials produced in one or more beneficiary countries and/or the direct costs of processing operations performed in one or more beneficiary countries. The Commonwealth of Puerto Rico and the U.S. Virgin Islands are defined as beneficiary countries for purposes of this requirement; therefore, value attributable to Puerto Rico or to the Virgin Islands may also be counted. In addition, the cost or value of materials produced in the customs territory of the United States (other than Puerto Rico) may be counted toward the 35 percent value-added requirement, but only to a maximum of 15 percent of the appraised value of the imported article.

The cost or value of materials imported into a beneficiary country from a non-beneficiary country may be included in calculating the 35 percent value-added requirement for an eligible article if the materials are first substantially transformed into new or different articles of commerce and are then used as constituent materials in the production of the eligible article. The phrase "direct costs of processing operations" includes costs directly incurred or reasonably allocated to the production of the article, such as the cost of actual labor, dies, molds, tooling, depreciation of machinery, research and development, inspection, and testing. Business overhead, administrative expenses and profit, as well as general business expenses such as casualty and liability insurance, advertising, and salespeople's salaries, are not considered direct costs of processing operations.

CBI II SECTION 215 AND 222

In addition to the origin rules enumerated above, the Customs and Trade Act of 1990 added new criteria for duty-free eligibility under the Caribbean Basin Initiative. First, articles which are the growth, product or manufacture of Puerto Rico and which subsequently are processed in a CBI beneficiary country may also receive duty-free treatment when entered, if the three following conditions are met:

- They are imported directly from a beneficiary country into the customs territory of the United States.
- They are advanced in value or improved in condition by any means in a beneficiary country.
- Any materials added to the article in a beneficiary country must be a product of a beneficiary country or the U.S.

Second, articles that are assembled or processed in whole from U.S. components or ingredients (other than water) in a beneficiary country may be entered free of duty. Duty-free treatment will apply if the components or ingredients are exported directly to the beneficiary country and the finished article is imported directly into the customs territory of the United States.

If advance tariff classification information is needed to ascertain whether your merchandise would be eligible for CBI duty-free treatment, you may obtain this information under the procedures previously discussed in Chapter 13 relating to dutiable status.

SOURCES OF ADDITIONAL INFORMATION

Customs rules and regulations on the CBI are incorporated in sections 10.191-10.198 of the Customs Regulations. Address any question you may have about the administrative or operational aspects of the CBI to the port director where the merchandise will be entered or to Director, Trade Compliance Division, U.S. Customs Service, Washington, DC 20229.

19. ANDEAN TRADE PREFERENCE ACT (ATPA)

The Andean Trade Preference Act (ATPA) is a program providing for the duty-free entry of certain merchandise from designated beneficiary countries. The ATPA was enacted into law by the United States on December 4, 1991, and is scheduled to expire on December 4, 2001.

BENEFICIARY COUNTRIES

The following countries have been designated as beneficiary countries for purposes of the ATPA:

Bolivia   Colombia   Ecuador   Peru

ELIGIBLE ITEMS

Most products from designated beneficiary countries may be eligible for ATPA duty-free treatment. Products that are statutorily excluded include: textile and apparel articles which are subject to textile agreements; some footwear; preserved tuna in airtight containers; petroleum products; watches and watch parts from countries subject to Column 2 rates of duty; various sugar products; rum and tafia. Eligible items are identified by either a "J" or "J*" in the "Special" subcolumn under column 1 of the Harmonized Tariff Schedule. Merchandise classifiable under a subheading designated in this manner may qualify for duty-free entry if imported into the United States directly from any designated ATPA beneficiary country. Merchandise from one or more of these countries, however, may be excluded from duty-free treatment if there is a "J*" in the "Special" subcolumn.

RULES OF ORIGIN

For commercial shipments requiring formal entry, a claim for preferential tariff treatment under ATPA is made by showing that the country of origin is a designated beneficiary country and by using the letter "J" as a prefix to the appropriate tariff schedule number on Customs Form 7501. Merchandise will be eligible for ATPA duty-free treatment only if the following conditions are met:

- The merchandise must have been produced in a beneficiary country. This requirement is satisfied when: (1) the goods are wholly the growth, product, or manufacture of a beneficiary country, or (2) the goods have been substantially transformed into a new or different article of commerce in a beneficiary country.

- The merchandise must be imported directly from any beneficiary country into the customs territory of the United States.

- At least 35 percent of the article's appraised value must consist of the cost or value of materials produced in one or more ATPA or CBI beneficiary countries and/or the direct costs of processing operations performed in one or more ATPA or CBI beneficiary countries. The Commonwealth of Puerto Rico and the U.S. Virgin Islands are defined as beneficiary countries for purposes of this requirement; therefore, value attributable to Puerto Rico or to the Virgin Islands may also be counted. In addition, the cost or value of materials produced in the customs territory of the United States (other than Puerto Rico) may be counted toward the 35 percent value-added requirement, but only to a maximum of 15 percent of the appraised value of the imported article.

The cost or value of materials imported into ATPA or CBI beneficiary countries from nonbeneficiary countries may be included in calculating the 35 percent value-added requirement for an eligible article if the materials are first substantially transformed into new or different articles of commerce and are then used as constituent materials in the production of the eligible article. The phrase "direct costs of processing operations" includes costs directly incurred or reasonably allocated to the production of the article, such as the cost of actual labor, dies, molds, tooling, depreciation of machinery, research and development, inspection and testing. Business overhead, administrative expenses and profit, as well as general business expenses such as casualty and liability insurance, advertising and salespersons' salaries are not considered direct costs of processing operations. If advance tariff classification information is needed to ascertain whether your merchandise would be eligible for ATPA duty-free treatment, you may obtain this information under the procedures previously discussed in Chapter 13 relating to dutiable status.

SOURCES OF ADDITIONAL INFORMATION

Address any questions you may have about the operational or administrative aspects of the ATPA to the Director, Trade Compliance Division, U.S. Customs Service, Washington, DC 20229.

20. U.S./ISRAEL FREE TRADE AREA AGREEMENT

The United States-Israel Free Trade Area (FTA) agreement is a program originally enacted to provide for duty-free treatment for merchandise produced in Israel to stimulate trade between the two countries. This program was authorized by the United States in the Trade and Tariff Act of 1984, became effective September 1, 1985, and has no termination date.

The FTA Implementation Act was amended on October 2, 1996, authorizing the President to implement certain changes affecting the duty status of goods from the West Bank, Gaza Strip, and qualifying industrial zones (QIZs). By Presidential Proclamation 6955 of November 13, 1996, General Note 3(v) was created to implement the new program for these goods. Pursuant to General Note 3(v), duty-free treatment is allowed for products of the West Bank, Gaza Strip, or a QIZ, imported directly from the West Bank, Gaza Strip, a QIZ or Israel, provided certain requirements are met. Also as a result of Presidential Proclamation 6955, the eligibility requirements were modified for duty-free treatment of articles which are the product of Israel.

ELIGIBLE ITEMS

The FTA relates to most tariff items listed in the Harmonized Tariff Schedule of the United States. These items are identified by "IL" in the *Special* column under column 1 of the Harmonized Tariff Schedule. If a claim for duty-free or reduced-duty rates is being made for commercial shipments of Israeli goods covered by a formal entry, the HTS subheading must be prefixed with an "IL" on Customs Form 7501 (entry document) or Customs Form 7505 (warehouse withdrawal document), as appropriate.

PRODUCTS OF ISRAEL

An article imported into the Customs territory of the United States is eligible for treatment as "Product of Israel" only if:

■ The merchandise has been produced in Israel. This requirement is satisfied when (1) the goods are wholly the growth, product, or manufacture of Israel, or (2) the goods have been substantially transformed into a new or different article of commerce in Israel;

■ That article is imported directly from Israel, the West Bank, Gaza Strip, or a QIZ into the customs territory of the United States;

■ The sum of: (1) the cost or value of the materials produced in Israel, the West Bank, Gaza Strip, or a QIZ, plus (2) the direct costs of processing operations performed in Israel, the West Bank, Gaza Strip, or a QIZ is not less than 35 percent of the appraised value of such article at the time it is entered. If the cost or value of materials produced in the customs territory of the United States is included with respect to an eligible article, an amount not to exceed 15 percent of the appraised value of the article at the time it is entered that is attributable to such United States cost or value may be applied toward determining the 35 percent.

PRODUCTS OF WEST BANK, GAZA STRIP, OR QUALIFYING INDUSTRIAL ZONE (QIZ)

An article imported into the customs territory of the United States is eligible for treatment as a product of the West Bank, Gaza Strip, or a QIZ only if:

- That article is the growth, product, or manufacture fo the West Bank, Gaza Strip or a QIZ.
- That article is imported directly from the West Bank, Gaza Strip, a QIZ or Israel into the customs territory of the United States.
- The sum of: (1) the cost or value of the materials produced in the West Bank, Gaza Strip, a QIZ or Israel, plus (2) the direct costs of processing operations performed in the West Bank, Gaza Strip, a QIZ or Israel, is not less than 35 percent of the appraised value of such article at the time it is entered. If the cost or value of materials produced in the customs territory of the United States is included with respect to an eligible article, an amount not to exceed 15 percent of the appraised value of the article at the time it is entered that is attributable to such United States cost or value may be applied toward the 35 percent.

No article may be considered to meet these requirements by virtue of having undergone:

- Simple combining or packaging operations; or
- Mere diluting with water or another substance that does not materially alter the characteristics of the article.

The phrase "direct costs of processing operations" includes, but is not limited to:

- All actual labor costs involved in the growth, production, manufacture or assembly of the specific merchandise, including fringe benefits, on-the-job training and the costs of engineering, supervisory, quality control and similar personnel.
- Dies, molds, tooling and depreciation on machinery and equipment which are allocable to the specific merchandise.

Direct costs of processing operations do not include costs which are not directly attributable to the merchandise concerned, or are not costs of manufacturing the product, such as (1) profit and (2) general expenses of doing business which are either not allocable to the specific merchandise or are not related to the growth, production, manufacture or assembly of the merchandise, such as administrative salaries, casualty and liability insurance, advertising and sales staff salaries, commissions or expenses.

CERTIFICATE OF ORIGIN FORM A

The United Nations Conference on Trade and Development (UNCTAD) Certificate of Origin Form A is used as documentary evidence to support duty-free and reduced-rate claims for Israeli articles covered by a formal entry. It does not have to be produced at the time of entry, however, unless so requested by the Customs Service. The form A may be presented on an entry-by-entry basis or may be used as a blanket declaration for a period of 12 months. The Form A can be obtained from the Israeli authorizing issuing authority or from UNCTAD, DC 21100, New York, NY 10017, telephone (212) 963–6895.

INFORMAL ENTRIES

The Form A is not required for commercial or non-commercial shipments covered by an informal entry. However, the port director may require such other evidence of the country of origin as deemed necessary. With regard to merchandise accompanying the traveler, it should be noted that in order to avoid delays to passengers, the inspecting Customs officer will extend Israeli duty-free or reduced-rate treatment to all eligible articles when satisfied, from the facts available, that the merchandise concerned is a product of Israel. In such cases, Form A is not required for the merchandise.

SOURCES OF ADDITIONAL INFORMATION

Address any questions you may have about the administrative or operational aspects of the FTA to the Director, Trade Compliance Division, U.S. Customs Service, Washington, DC 20229. Requests for information concerning policy issues related to the FTA should be directed to the Chairman, Trade Policy Staff Subcommittee, Office of U.S. Trade Representative, 600 17th St., NW, Washington, DC 20506.

21. COMPACT OF FREE ASSOCIATION (FAS)

FAS is a program providing for the duty-free entry of certain merchandise from designated freely associated states. This program, established by Presidential Proclamation 6030 of September 28, 1989, Section 242, became effective on October 18, 1989 and has no termination date.

BENEFICIARY COUNTRIES

The following freely associated states have been designated as beneficiary countries for purposes of the FAS:

Marshall Islands

Federated States of Micronesia

Republic of Palau

ELIGIBLE ITEMS

The duty-free treatment is applied to most products from the designated beneficiaries. For commercial shipments requiring formal entry, a claim for duty-free status is made by placing the letter "Z" next to the eligible subheading. The following merchandise is excluded from the duty-free exemption:

- Textile and apparel articles that are subject to textile agreements.
- Footwear, handbags, luggage, flat goods, work gloves, and leather wearing apparel that were not eligible for GSP treatment, discussed in Chapter 17, on April 1, 1984.
- Watches, clocks, and timing apparatus of Chapter 91 of the Harmonized Tariff Schedule (except such articles incorporating an optoelectronic display and no other type of display).

- Buttons of subheading 9606.21.40 or 9606.29.20 of the Harmonized Tariff Schedule.
- Tuna and skipjack, prepared or preserved, not in oil, in airtight containers weighing with their contents not more than 7 kilograms each, *"in excess"* of the consumption quota quantity allowed duty-free entry.
- Any agricultural product of Chapters 2 through 52 inclusive, that is subject to a tariff-rate quota, if entered in a quantity in excess of the in-quota quantity for such products.

RULES OF ORIGIN

Merchandise will be eligible for FAS duty-free treatment only if the following conditions are met:

- The merchandise must have been produced in the freely associated state. This requirement is satisfied when (1) the goods are wholly the growth, product, or manufacture of the freely associated state, or (2) the goods have been substantially transformed into a new or different article of commerce in the freely associated state.
- The merchandise must be imported directly from the freely associated state into the customs territory of the United States.
- At least 35 percent of the appraised value of the article imported into the United States must consist of the cost or value of materials produced in the beneficiary country. In addition, the cost or value of materials produced in the customs territory of the

United States may be counted toward the 35 percent value-added requirement, but only to a maximum of 15 percent of the appraised value of the imported article. The cost or value of the materials imported into the freely associated state from a non-beneficiary country may be included in calculating the 35 percent value-added requirement for an eligible article if the materials are first substantially transformed into new or different articles of commerce and are then used as constituent materials in the production of the eligible product.

SOURCES OF ADDITIONAL INFORMATION

Address any questions you may have about the administrative or operational aspects of the FAS to the port director where the merchandise will be entered or to the Director, Trade Compliance Division, U.S. Customs Service, Washington, DC 20229.

22. ANTIDUMPING AND COUNTERVAILING DUTIES

Antidumping and countervailing duties are types of additional duties used to offset the effects of two unfair trade practices that give imports an unfair advantage over competing U.S. goods. Antidumping duties are assessed on imported merchandise that is sold, or is likely to be sold, in the United States at less than its fair value, which is the amount that the foreign market value exceeds the United States price of the merchandise. The foreign market value may be based on the price at which the merchandise is sold in the home market or to third countries, or on a constructed value (based on cost) of the merchandise. Countervailing duties are assessed to counter subsidies provided to merchandise that is exported to the United States. In addition to being subsidized or sold at less than fair value, the imported merchandise must also injure a U.S. industry (except for subsidized products from certain countries that are not entitled to an injury determination).

The Department of Commerce, the International Trade Commission (ITC), and the U.S. Customs Service all play a part in enforcing antidumping (AD) and countervailing duty (CVD) laws. The Commerce Department is also responsible for their general administration; it determines whether the merchandise is sold at less than fair value or is subsidized. It also determines the amount of duties that must be assessed. The ITC makes the injury determinations. The Customs Service assesses the duties once Commerce and the ITC have made the necessary determinations.

Establishing and assessing both kinds of duties occurs during the following processes:

Investigation. Although they may be initiated by the Commerce Department, AD and CVD investigations are usually initiated as the result of a petition from a domestic industry or another interested party such as a trade union or industry association. The party must simultaneously (that is, on the same day) file the petition with the Commerce Department and the ITC (the latter if an injury test is required).

If the necessary elements are present in the petition, the Commerce Department and the ITC will initiate separate investigations. The investigations then continue with a series of preliminary and final determinations that, if appropriate, result in an "order" and the eventual assessment of AD and CVD duties. The following discussion is based on the assumption that the injury test is required. If not, the outcome of the considerations is based solely on the Commerce Department determinations.

The ITC makes the first preliminary determination concerning the likelihood of injury. If that determination is negative, the investigations are terminated. If it is affirmative, the Commerce Department then issues a preliminary determination with respect to the sales and/or subsidy issues. Later, based on further review and comments received in the case, the Commerce Department issues a final determination. If either of these Commerce Department determinations is affirmative, Commerce will direct Customs to suspend liquidation of entries for merchandise subject to investigation and to require cash deposits or bonds equal to the amount of estimated dumping margin (the differential between the fair market value and the U.S. price) or the net subsidy.

After a final affirmative determination by the Commerce Department, the ITC the follows with its final injury determination. If the ITC's final determination is also affirmative, the Commerce Department issues an AD or CVD order. At that time, Commerce directs Customs to require, with a very limited exception for new shippers, only cash deposits of estimated duties. A negative final determination either by Commerce or the ITC would terminate the investigations. Both agencies announce their determinations, including orders and the results of the administration reviews described below, in the *Federal Register*

Administration Review/Liquidation. Each year, in the anniversary month of the order, interested parties have the opportunity to request a review of the order with respect to individual producers or resellers covered by an order. The period of review is usually the 12 months preceding the anniversary month. However, the first review period also includes any term prior to the normal 12-month period for which the suspension of liquidation was directed. If no review is requested, Commerce will direct Customs to assess duties in the amount of the cash or bond rate in effect at the time of entry summary filing and to continue to require deposits at that rate for future entries. If a review is requested, Commerce carries out a review similar to its original investigation and issues revised rates for assessment and deposits. Upon receipt of instructions from the Commerce Department, Customs will then liquidate the entries and make refunds or collect additional duties as appropriate.

23. DRAWBACK—REFUNDS OF DUTIES

DEFINITION AND PURPOSE

The term *drawback* refers to a refund of 99 percent of the duties or taxes collected on imported merchandise because certain legal or regulatory requirements have been met. To qualify for drawback, an importation of merchandise and subsequent exportation or destruction of merchandise must occur. The purpose of the drawback program is to assist American importers, manufacturers and exporters to compete in international markets by allowing them to obtain refunds of duties paid on imported merchandise.

THREE TYPES OF DRAWBACK

There are three primary types of drawback—manufacturing drawback, unused-merchandise drawback and rejected-merchandise drawback:

- **Manufacturing drawback** is a refund of duties paid on imported merchandise used in the manufacture of articles that are either exported or destroyed. The imported merchandise must be used in manufacture and exported within five years from the date of importation of the merchandise. An approved drawback ruling (formerly called a drawback contract) must be on file with Customs before any manufacturing drawback claims are filed.

- **Unused-merchandise drawback** is a refund of duties paid on imported merchandise that is exported or destroyed without undergoing manufacture, and is never used in the United States. The imported merchandise must be exported within three years from the date of importation of the merchandise.

■ **Rejected-merchandise drawback** is refund of duties on imported merchandise that is exported because it did not conform to sample or specifications, or was shipped without the consent of the consignee. Merchandise must be returned to Customs custody within three years of the date of its importation in order to qualify for this type of drawback. Rejected merchandise must be exported and cannot be destroyed in lieu of such exportation.

These drawback claims involve a refund of 99 percent of the duties that were paid upon importation. The drawback regulations may be found in Part 191 of the Customs Regulations.

Questions about drawback should be addressed to:

Chief, Drawback Unit
Office of Field Operations
U.S. Customs Service
1300 Pennsylvania Avenue NW
Washington, DC 20229.

24. CLASSIFICATION—LIQUIDATION

CLASSIFICATION

Classification and, when ad valorem rates of duty are applicable, appraisement, are the two most important factors affecting dutiable status. Classification and valuation, whether or not they are pertinent because an ad valorem rate of duty applies, must be provided by commercial importers when an entry is filed. In addition, classifications under the statistical suffixes of the tariff schedules must also be furnished even though this information is not pertinent to dutiable status. Accordingly, classification is initially the responsibility of an importer, customs broker or other person preparing the entry papers. Section 637 of the Customs Modernization Act imposes the requirement that importers exercise reasonable care when classifying and appraising merchandise.

Familiarity with the organization of the Harmonized Tariff Schedule of the United States facilitates the classification process. (See Chapter 13 of this booklet relating to dutiable status.) The tariff schedule is divided into various sections and chapters dealing separately with merchandise in broad product categories. These categories cover animal products, vegetable products, products of various basic materials such as wood, textiles, plastics, rubber, and steel and other metal products in various stages of manufacture, for example. Other sections encompass chemicals, machinery and electrical equipment, and other specified or non-enumerated products. The last section, Section XXII, covers certain exceptions from duty and special statutory provisions.

In Sections I through XXI, products are classifiable (1) under items or descriptions which name them, known as an *eo nomine* provision; (2) under provisions of general description; (3) under provisions which identify them by component material, or (4) under provisions which encompass merchandise in accordance with its actual or principal use. When two or more provisions seem to cover the same merchandise, the prevailing provision is determined in accordance with the legal notes and the General Rules of Interpretation for the tariff schedule. Also applicable are tariff classification principles contained in administrative precedents or in the case law of the U.S. Court of International Trade (formerly the U.S. Customs Court) or the U.S. Court of Appeals for the Federal Circuit (formerly the U.S. Court of Customs and Patent Appeals).

LIQUIDATION

Customs officers at the port of entry or other officials acting on behalf of the port director review selected classifications and valuations, as well as other required import information, for correctness or as a proper basis for appraisement, as well as for agreement of the submitted data with the merchandise actually imported. The entry summary and documentation may be accepted as submitted without any changes. In this situation, the entry is liquidated as entered. Liquidation is the point at which the Customs Service's ascertainment of the rate and amount of duty becomes final for most purposes. Liquidation is accomplished by posting a notice on a public bulletin board at the customs house. However, an importer may receive an advance notice on Customs Form 4333A "Courtesy Notice" stating when and in what amount duty will be liquidated. This form is not the liquidation, and protest rights do not accrue until the notice is posted. Time limits for protesting do not start until the date of posting, and a protest cannot be filed before liquidation is posted.

The Customs Service may determine that an entry cannot be liquidated as entered for one reason or another. For example, the tariff classification may not be correct or may not be acceptable because it is not consistent with established and uniform classification practice. If the change required by this determination results in a rate of duty more favorable to an importer, the entry is liquidated accordingly and a refund is authorized for the applicable amount of the deposited estimated duties. On the other hand, a change may be necessary which imposes a higher rate of duty. For example, a claim for an exemption from duty under a free-rate provision or under a conditional exemption may be found to be insufficient for lack of the required supporting documentation. In this situation, the importer will be given an advance notice of the proposed duty rate increase and an opportunity to validate the claim for a free rate or more favorable rate of duty.

If the importer does not respond to the notice, or if the response is found to be without merit, entry is liquidated in accordance with the entry as corrected, and the importer is billed for the additional duty. The port may find that the importer's response raises issues of such complexity that resolution is warranted by a Customs Headquarters decision through the internal advice procedure. Internal advice from Customs Headquarters may be requested by local Customs officers on their own initiative or in response to a request by the importer.

PROTESTS

After liquidation, an importer may still pursue, on Customs Form 19 (19 CFR 174), any claims for an adjustment or refund by filing a protest within 90 days after liquidation. In order to apply for a Headquarters ruling, a request for further review must be filed with the protest. The same Form 19 can be used for this purpose. If filed separately, application for further review must still be filed within 90 days of liquidation. However, if a ruling on the question has previously been issued in response to a request for a decision on a prospective transaction or a request for internal advice, further review will ordinarily be denied. If a protest is denied, an importer has the right to litigate the matter by filing a summons with the U.S. Court of International Trade within 180 days after denial of the protest. The rules of the court and other applicable statutes and precedents determine the course of customs litigation.

While the Customs Service's ascertainment of dutiable status is final for most purposes at the time of liquidation, a liquidation is not final until any protest which has been filed against it has been decided. Similarly, the administrative decision issued on a protest is not final until any litigation filed against it has become final.

Entries must be liquidated within one year of the date of entry unless the liquidation needs to be extended for another one-year period not to exceed a total of four years from the date of entry. The Customs Service will suspend liquidation of an entry when required by statute or court order. A suspension will remain in effect until the issue is resolved. Notifications of extensions and suspensions are given to importers, surety companies and customs brokers who are parties to the transaction.

25. CONVERSION OF CURRENCY

The conversion of foreign currency for customs purposes must be made in accordance with the provisions of 31 U.S.C. 5151. This section states that Customs is to use rates of exchange determined and certified by the Federal Reserve Bank of New York. These certified rates are based on the New York market buying rates for the foreign currencies involved.

In the case of widely used currencies, rates of exchange are certified each day. The rates certified on the first business day of each calendar quarter are used throughout the quarter except on days when fluctuations of five percent or more occur, in which case the actual certified rates for those days are used. For infrequently used currencies, the Federal Reserve Bank of New York certifies rates of exchanges upon request by Customs. The rates certified are only for the currencies and dates requested.

For Customs purposes, the date of exportation of the goods is the date used to determine the applicable certified rate of exchange. This remains true even though a different rate may have been used in payment of the goods. Information as to the applicable rate of exchange in converting currency for customs purposes in the case of a given shipment may be obtained from a port director of Customs.

26. TRANSACTION VALUE

The entry filer is responsible for using reasonable care to value imported merchandise and provide any other information necessary to enable the Customs officer to properly assess the duty and determine whether any other applicable legal requirement is met. The Customs officer is then responsible for fixing the value of the imported merchandise. The valuation provisions of the Tariff Act of 1930 are found in section 402, as amended by the Trade Agreements Act of 1979. Pertinent portions are reproduced in the appendix.

Generally, the customs value of all merchandise exported to the United States will be the transaction value for the goods. If the transaction value cannot be used, then certain secondary bases are considered. The secondary bases of value, listed in order of precedence for use, are:

- Transaction value of identical merchandise.
- Transaction value of similar merchandise.
- Deductive value.
- Computed value.

The order of precedence of the last two values can be reversed if the importer so requests in writing at the time of filing the entry. These secondary bases are discussed in the next two chapters.

TRANSACTION VALUE

The transaction value of imported merchandise is the price actually paid or payable for the merchandise when sold for exportation to the United States, plus amounts for the following items if they are not included in the price:

- The packing costs incurred by the buyer.
- Any selling commission incurred by the buyer.
- The value of any assist.
- Any royalty or license fee that the buyer is required to pay as a condition of the sale.
- The proceeds, accruing to the seller, of any subsequent resale, disposal, or use of the imported merchandise.

The amounts for the above items are added only to the extent that each is not included in the price actually paid or payable and information is available to establish the accuracy of the amount. If sufficient information is not available, then the transaction value cannot be determined and the next basis of value, in order of precedence, must be considered for appraisement. A discussion of these added items follows:

Packing costs consist of the cost incurred by the buyer for all containers and coverings of whatever nature and for the labor and materials used in packing the imported merchandise so that it is ready for export.

Any selling commission incurred by the buyer with respect to the imported merchandise constitutes part of the transaction value. Buying commissions do not. A selling commission means any commission paid to the seller's agent, who is related to or controlled by, or works for or on behalf of, the manufacturer or the seller.

The apportioned value of any assist constitutes part of the transaction value of the imported merchandise. First the value of the assist is determined; then the value is prorated to the imported merchandise.

Assists. An assist is any of the items listed below that the buyer of imported merchandise provides directly or indirectly, free of charge or at a reduced cost, for use in the production or sale of merchandise for export to the United States.

- Materials, components, parts, and similar items incorporated in the imported merchandise.
- Tools, dies, molds, and similar items used in producing the imported merchandise.
- Merchandise consumed in producing the imported merchandise.
- Engineering, development, artwork, design work, and plans and sketches that are undertaken outside the United States.

"Engineering...," will not be treated as an assist if the service or work is (1) performed by a person domiciled within the United States, (2) performed while that person is acting as an employee or agent of the buyer of the imported merchandise, and (3) incidental to other engineering, development, artwork, design work, or plans or sketches undertaken within the United States.

Value. In determining the value of an assist, the following rules apply:

- The value is either (a) the cost of acquiring the assist, if acquired by the importer from an unrelated seller, or (b) the cost of the assist, if produced by the importer or a person related to the importer.
- The value includes the cost of transporting the assist to the place of production.
- The value of assists used in producing the imported merchandise is adjusted to reflect use, repairs, modifications, or other factors affecting the value of the assists. Assists of this type include such items as tools, dies and molds.

For example, if the importer previously used the assist, regardless of whether he acquired or produced it, the original cost of acquisition or of production must be decreased to reflect the use. Alternatively, repairs and modifications may result in the value of the assist having to be adjusted upward.

- In case of engineering, development, artwork, design work, and plans and sketches undertaken elsewhere than in the United States, the value is (a) the cost of obtaining copies of the assist, if the assist is available in the public domain; (b) the cost of the purchase or lease, if the assist was bought or leased by the buyer from an unrelated person; (c) the value added outside the United States, if the assist was reproduced in the United States and one or more foreign countries.

So far as possible, the buyer's commercial record system will be used to determine the value of an assist, especially such assists as engineering, development, artwork, design work, and plans and sketches undertaken elsewhere than in the United States.

Apportionment. Having determined the value of an assist, the next step is to prorate that value to the imported merchandise. The apportionment is done in a reasonable manner appropriate to the circumstances and in accordance with generally accepted accounting principles. By the latter is meant any generally recognized consensus or substantial authoritative support regarding the recording and measuring of assets and liabilities and changes, the disclosing of information, and the preparing of financial statements.

Royalty or license fees that a buyer must pay directly or indirectly as a condition of the sale of the imported merchandise for exportation to the United States will be included in the transaction value. Ultimately, whether a royalty or license fee is dutiable will depend on whether the buyer had to pay it as a condition of the sale and to whom and under what circumstances it was paid. The dutiability status will have to be decided on a case-by-case basis.

Charges for the right to reproduce the imported goods in the United States are not dutiable. This right applies only to the following types of merchandise:

- Originals or copies of artistic or scientific works.

- Originals or copies of models and industrial drawings.

- Model machines and prototypes.

- Plant and animal species.

Any proceeds resulting from the subsequent resale, disposal, or use of the imported merchandise that accrue, directly or indirectly, to the seller are dutiable. These proceeds are added to the price actually paid or payable if not otherwise included.

The price actually paid or payable for the imported merchandise is the total payment, excluding international freight, insurance, and other c.i.f. charges, that the buyer makes to the seller. This payment may be direct or indirect. Some examples of an indirect payment are when the buyer settles all or part of a debt owed by the seller, or when the seller reduces the price on a current importation to settle a debt he owes the buyer. Such indirect payments are part of the transaction value.

However, if a buyer performs an activity on his own account, other than those which may be included in the transaction value, then the activity is not considered an indirect payment to the seller and is not part of the transaction value. This applies even though the buyer's activity might be regarded as benefiting the seller; for example, advertising.

EXCLUSIONS

The amounts to be excluded from transaction value are as follows:

- The cost, charges, or expenses incurred for transportation, insurance, and related services incident to the international shipment of the goods from the country of exportation to the place of importation in the United States.

- Any reasonable cost or charges incurred for:

   1. Constructing, erecting, assembling, maintaining, or providing technical assistance with respect to the goods after importation into the United States, or

   2. Transporting the goods after importation.

- The customs duties and other federal taxes, including any federal excise tax, for which sellers in the United States are ordinarily liable.

NOTE: Foreign inland freight and related charges in bullet 1 (see part 152, Customs Regulations), as well as bullets 2 and 3 above, must be identified separately.

LIMITATIONS

The transaction value of imported merchandise is the appraised value of that merchandise, provided certain limitations do not exist. If any of these limitations are present, then transaction value cannot be used as the appraised value, and the next basis of value will be considered. The limitations can be divided into four groups:

- Restrictions on the disposition or use of the merchandise.

- Conditions for which a value cannot be determined.

- Proceeds of any subsequent resale, disposal or use of the merchandise, accruing to the seller, for which an appropriate adjustment to transaction value cannot be made.

- Related-party transactions where the transaction value is not acceptable.

The term "acceptable" means that the relationship between the buyer and seller did not influence the price actually paid or payable.

Examining the circumstances of the sale will help make this determination.

Alternatively, "acceptable" can also mean that the transaction value of the imported merchandise closely approximates one of the following test values, provided these values relate to merchandise exported to the United States at or about the same time as the imported merchandise:

■ The transaction value of identical merchandise or of similar merchandise in sales to unrelated buyers in the United States.

■ The deductive value or computed value for identical merchandise or similar merchandise. The test values are used for comparison only; they do not form a substitute basis of valuation.

In determining whether the transaction value is close to one of the foregoing test values, an adjustment is made if the sales involved differ in:

■ Commercial levels,

■ Quantity levels,

■ The costs, commission, values, fees, and proceeds added to the transaction value (price paid) if not included in the price, and

■ The costs incurred by the seller in sales in which he and the buyer are not related that are not incurred by the seller in sales in which he and the buyer are related.

As stated, the test values are alternatives to the relationship criterion. If one of the test values is met, it is not necessary to examine the question of whether the relationship influenced the price.

27. TRANSACTION VALUE OF IDENTICAL MERCHANDISE OR SIMILAR MERCHANDISE

When the transaction value cannot be determined, then the customs value of the imported goods being appraised is the transaction value of identical merchandise. If merchandise identical to the imported goods cannot be found or an acceptable transaction value for such merchandise does not exist, then the customs value is the transaction value of similar merchandise. The above value would be a previously accepted customs value.

Besides the data common to all three transaction values, certain factors specifically apply to the transaction value of identical merchandise or similar merchandise. These factors concern (1) the exportation date, (2) the level and quantity of sales, (3) the meaning, and (4) the order of precedence of identical merchandise and of similar merchandise.

Exportation date. The identical (similar) merchandise for which a value is being determined must have been exported to the United States at or about the same time that the merchandise being appraised is exported to the United States.

Sales Level/Quantity. The transaction value of identical (similar) merchandise must be based on sales of identical (similar) merchandise at the same commercial level and in substantially the same quantity as the sale of the merchandise being appraised. If no such sale exists, then sales at either a different commercial level or in different quantities, or both, can be used but must be adjusted to take account of any such difference. Any adjustment must be based on sufficient information, that is, information establishing the reasonableness and accuracy of the adjustment.

Meanings. The term "identical merchandise" means merchandise that is:

■ Identical in all respects to the merchandise being appraised.

■ Produced in the same country as the merchandise being appraised.

- Produced by the same person as the merchandise being appraised.

  If merchandise meeting all three criteria cannot be found, then identical merchandise is merchandise satisfying the first two criteria but produced by a different person than the producer of merchandise being appraised.

NOTE: Merchandise can be identical to the merchandise being appraised and still show minor differences in appearance.

- Exclusion: Identical merchandise does not include merchandise that incorporates or reflects engineering, development, art work, design work, and plans and sketches provided free or at reduced cost by the buyer and undertaken in the United States.

  The term "similar merchandise" means merchandise that is:

- Produced in the same country and by the same person as the merchandise being appraised.

- Like the merchandise being appraised in characteristics and component materials.

- Commercially interchangeable with the merchandise being appraised.

  If merchandise meeting the foregoing criteria cannot be found, then similar merchandise is merchandise having the same country of production, like characteristics and component materials, and commercial interchangeability but produced by a different person.

  In determining whether goods are similar, some of the factors to be considered are the quality of the goods, their reputation, and existence of a trademark.

- Exclusion: Similar merchandise does not include merchandise that incorporates or reflects engineering, development, art work, design work, and plans and sketches provided free or at reduced cost to the buyer and undertaken in the United States.

Order of Precedence. It is possible that two or more transaction values for identical (similar) merchandise will be determined. In such a case the lowest value will be used as the appraised value of the imported merchandise.

28. OTHER BASES: DEDUCTIVE AND COMPUTED VALUE

DEDUCTIVE VALUE

If the transaction value of imported merchandise, of identical merchandise, or of similar merchandise cannot be determined, then deductive value is calculated for the merchandise being appraised. Deductive value is the next basis of appraisement at the time the entry summary is filed, to be used unless the importer designates computed value as the preferred method of appraisement. If computed value was chosen and subsequently determined not to exist for customs valuation purposes, then the basis of appraisement reverts to deductive value.

If an assist is involved in a sale, that sale cannot be used in determining deductive value. So any sale to a person who supplies an assist for use in connection with the production or sale for export of the merchandise concerned

is disregarded for purposes of determining deductive value.

Basically, deductive value is the resale price in the United States after importation of the goods, with deductions for certain items. In discussing deductive value, the term "merchandise concerned" is used. The term means the merchandise being appraised, identical merchandise, or similar merchandise. Generally, the deductive value is calculated by starting with a unit price and making certain additions to and deductions from that price.

Unit Price. One of three prices constitutes the unit price in deductive value. The price used depends on when and in what condition the merchandise concerned is sold in the United States.

1. **Time and Condition:** The merchandise is *sold in the condition as imported at or about the*

date of importation of the merchandise being appraised.

Price: The price used is the unit price at which the greatest aggregate quantity of the merchandise concerned is sold at or about the date of importation.

2. Time and Condition: The merchandise concerned is *sold in the condition as imported but not sold at or about the date of importation* of the merchandise being appraised.

Price: The price used is the unit price at which the greatest aggregate quantity of the merchandise concerned is sold after the date of importation of the merchandise being appraised but before the close of the 90th day after the date of importation.

3. Time and Condition: The merchandise concerned is *not sold in the condition as imported and not sold before the close of the 90th day* after the date of importation of the merchandise being appraised.

Price: The price used is the unit price at which the greatest aggregate quantity of the merchandise being appraised, after further processing, is sold before the 180th day after the date of importation.

This third price is also known as the "further processing price" or "superdeductive."

Additions. Packing costs for the merchandise concerned are added to the price used for deductive value, provided these costs have not otherwise been included. These costs are added regardless of whether the importer or the buyer incurs the cost. "Packing costs" means the cost of:

- All containers and coverings of whatever nature; and

- Packing, whether for labor or materials, used in placing the merchandise in condition, packed ready for shipment to the United States.

Deductions. Certain items are not part of deductive value and must be deducted from the unit price. These items are as follows:

- **Commissions or Profit and General Expenses.** Any commission usually paid or agreed to be paid, or the addition usually

made for profit and general expenses, applicable to sales in the United States of imported merchandise that is of the same class or kind as the merchandise concerned, regardless of the country of exportation.

- **Transportation/Insurance Costs.** The usual and associated costs of transporting and insuring the merchandise concerned from (a) the country of exportation to the place of importation in the United States, and (b) the place of importation to the place of delivery in the United States, provided these costs are not included as a general expense under the preceding item 1.

- **Customs Duties/Federal Taxes.** The customs duties and other federal taxes payable on the merchandise concerned because of its importation plus any federal excise tax on, or measured by the value of, such merchandise for which sellers in the United States are ordinarily liable.

- **Value of Further Processing.** The value added by processing the merchandise after importation, provided that sufficient information exists concerning the cost of processing. The price determined for deductive value is reduced by the value of further processing only if the third unit price (the superdeductive) is used as deductive value.

Superdeductive. The importer has the option to ask that deductive value be based on the further processing price. If the importer makes that choice, certain facts concerning valuing the further-processing method, termed "superdeductive," must be followed.

Under the superdeductive method the merchandise concerned is *not sold in the condition as imported* and *not sold before the close of the 90th day* after the date of importation, but is sold before the 180th day after the date of importation.

Under this method, an amount equal to the value of the further processing must be deducted from the unit price in determining deductive value. The amount so deducted must be based on objective and quantifiable data concerning the cost of such work as well as any spoilage, waste or scrap derived from that work. Items such as accepted industry formulas, methods of construction, and industry practices could be used as a basis for calculating the amount to be deducted.

Generally, the superdeductive method cannot be used if the further processing destroys the identity of the goods. Such situations will be decided on a case-by-case basis for the following reasons:

■ Sometimes, even though the identity of the goods is lost, the value added by the processing can be determined accurately without unreasonable difficulty for importers or for the Customs Service.

■ In some cases, the imported goods still keep their identity after processing but form only a minor part of the goods sold in the United States. In such cases, using the superdeductive method to value the imported goods will not be justified.

The superdeductive method cannot be used if the merchandise concerned is sold in the condition as imported before the close of the 90th day after the date of importation of the merchandise being appraised.

COMPUTED VALUE

The next basis of appraisement is computed value. If customs valuation cannot be based on any of the values previously discussed, then computed value is considered. This value is also the one the importer can select to precede deductive value as a basis of appraisement.

Computed value consists of the sum of the following items:

■ Materials, fabrication, and other processing used in producing the imported merchandise.

■ Profit and general expenses.

■ Any assist, if not included in bullets 1 and 2.

■ Packing costs.

Materials, Fabrication, and Other Processing. The cost or value of the materials, fabrication, and other processing of any kind used in producing the imported merchandise is based on (a) information provided by or on behalf of the producer, and (b) the commercial accounts of the producer if the accounts are consistent with

generally accepted accounting principles applied in the country of production of the goods.

NOTE: If the country of exportation imposes an internal tax on the materials or their disposition and refunds the tax when merchandise produced from the materials is exported, then the amount of the internal tax is not included as part of the cost or value of the materials.

Profit and General Expenses. The producer's profit and general expenses are used, provided they are consistent with the usual profit and general expenses reflected by producers in the country of exportation in sales of merchandise of the same class or kind as the imported merchandise. Some facts concerning the amount for profit and general expenses should be mentioned:

■ The amount is determined by information supplied by the producer and is based on his or her commercial accounts, provided such accounts are consistent with generally accepted accounting principles in the country of production.

NOTE: As a point of contrast, for deductive value the generally accepted accounting principles used are those in the United States, whereas in computed value the generally accepted accounting principles are those in the country of production.

■ The producer's profit and general expenses must be consistent with those usually reflected in sales of goods of the same class or kind as the imported merchandise that are made by producers in the country of exportation for export to the United States. If they are not consistent, then the amount for profit and general expenses is based on the usual profit and general expenses of such producers.

■ The amount for profit and general expenses is taken as a whole. This is the same treatment as occurs in deductive value.

Basically, a producer's profit could be low and his or her general expenses high, so that the total amount is consistent with that usually reflected in sales of goods of the same class or kind. In such a situation, a producer's actual profit figures, even if low, will be used provided he or she has valid commercial reasons to justify them and the pricing policy reflects usual pricing policies in the industry concerned.

Assists. If the value of an assist used in producing the merchandise is not included as part of the producer's materials, fabrication, other processing, or general expenses, then the prorated value of the assist will be included in computed value. It is important that the value of the assist not be included elsewhere because no component of computed value should be counted more than once in determining computed value.

NOTE: The value of any engineering, development, artwork, design work, and plans and sketches undertaken in the United States is included in computed value only to the extent that such value has been charged to the producer.

Packing Costs. The cost of all containers and coverings of whatever nature, and of packing, whether for labor or material, used in placing merchandise in condition and packed ready for shipment to the United States is included in computed value.

Under computed value, "merchandise of the same class or kind" must be imported from the same country as the merchandise being appraised and must be within a group or range of goods produced by a particular industry or industry sector. Whether certain merchandise is of the same class or kind as other merchandise will be determined on a case-by-case basis.

In determining usual profit and general expenses, sales for export to the United States of the narrowest group or range of merchandise that includes the merchandise being appraised will be examined, providing that the necessary information can be obtained.

NOTE: As a point of contrast, under deductive value, "merchandise of the same class or kind" includes merchandise imported from other countries besides the country from which the merchandise being appraised was imported.

Under computed value, "merchandise of the same class or kind" is limited to merchandise imported from the same country as the merchandise being appraised.

VALUE IF OTHER VALUES CANNOT BE DETERMINED

If none of the previous five values can be used to appraise the imported merchandise, then the customs value must be based on a value derived from one of the five previous methods, reasonably adjusted as necessary. The value so determined should be based, to the greatest extent possible, on previously determined values. In order for Customs to consider an importer's argument regarding appraisement, the information upon which the argument is based must be made available to Customs, whether it was generated by a foreign or domestic source. Some examples of how the other methods can be reasonably adjusted are:

- Identical Merchandise (or Similar Merchandise):

  1. The requirement that the identical merchandise (or similar merchandise) should be exported at or about the same time as the merchandise being appraised could be flexibly interpreted.

  2. Identical imported merchandise (or similar imported merchandise) produced in a country other than the country of exportation of the merchandise being appraised could be the basis for customs valuation.

  3. Customs values of identical imported merchandise (or similar imported merchandise) already determined on the basis of deductive value and computed value could be used.

- Deductive Method: The 90-day requirement may be administered flexibly (19 CFR 152.107(c)).

MARKING

29. COUNTRY OF ORIGIN MARKING

United States customs laws require each imported article produced abroad to be marked in a conspicuous place as legibly, indelibly, and permanently as the nature of the article permits, with the English name of the country of origin, to indicate to the ultimate purchaser in the United States the name of the country in which the article was manufactured or produced. Articles which are otherwise specifically exempted from individual marking are an exception to this rule. The exceptions are discussed below.

MARKING REQUIRED

If the article (or the container when the container and not the article must be marked) is not properly marked at the time of importation, a marking duty equal to 10 percent of the customs value of the article will be assessed unless the article is exported, destroyed, or properly marked under Customs supervision before the liquidation of the entry concerned.

It is not feasible to state who will be the "ultimate purchaser" in every circumstance. Broadly stated, an "ultimate purchaser" may be defined as the last person in the United States who will receive the article in the form in which it was imported. Generally, if an imported article will be used in the United States in manufacture that results in an article having a name, character or usage different from that of the imported article, the manufacturer is the ultimate purchaser. If an article is to be sold at retail in its imported form, the purchaser at retail is the ultimate purchaser. A person who subjects an imported article to a process which results in a substantial transformation of the article is the ultimate purchaser, but if the process is merely a minor one which leaves the identity of the imported article intact, the processor of the article will not be regarded as the ultimate purchaser.

When an article (or its container) is required to be marked to indicate its country of origin, the marking is sufficiently permanent if it will remain on the article (or its container) until it reaches the ultimate purchaser. When an article is of a kind which is usually combined with another article subsequent to importation but before delivery to an ultimate purchaser, and the name indicating the article's country of origin appears in a place on the article so that the name will be visible after such combining, the marking shall include, in addition to the name of the country of origin, words or symbols which clearly show that the origin indicated is that of the imported article only and not that of any other article with which the imported article may be combined after importation. For example, if marked bottles, drums, or other containers are imported empty, to be filled in the United States, they shall be marked with such words as "Bottle (or drum or container) made in (name of country)." Labels and similar articles so marked that the name of the article's country of origin is visible after it is affixed to another article in this country shall be marked with additional descriptive words such as "label made (or printed) in (name of country)" or words of similar import.

In any case in which the words "United States" or "American" or the letters "U.S.A." or any variation of such words or letters, or the name of any city or locality in the United States, or the name of any foreign country or locality in which the article was not manufactured or produced, appear on an imported article or container, there shall appear, legibly and permanently, in close proximity to such words, letters or name, the name of the country of origin preceded by "Made in," "Product of," or other words of similar meaning.

If marked articles are to be repacked in the United States after release from Customs custody, importers must certify on entry that they will not obscure the marking on properly marked articles if the article is repacked or that they will mark the repacked container. If the importers do not repack, but resell to repackers, importers must notify the repackers of the marking requirements. Failure to comply with the certification requirements may subject importers to penalties and/or additional duties.

MARKING NOT REQUIRED

The following articles and classes or kinds of articles are not required to be marked to indicate the country of their origin, i.e., the country in which they were grown, manufactured, or produced. However, the outermost containers in which these articles ordinarily reach the ultimate purchaser in the United States must be marked to indicate the English name of the country of origin of the articles.

Art, works of.
Articles classified subheads 9810.00 15, 9810 00.25, 9810.00.40, and 9810 00.45, HTSUS.
Articles entered in good faith as antiques and rejected as unauthentic.
Bagging, waste.
Bags, jute
Bands, steel.
Beads, unstrung.
Bearings, ball, 5/8-inch or less in diameter
Blanks, metal, to be plated.
Bodies, harvest hat.
Bolts, nuts, and washers
Briarwood, in blocks.
Briquettes, coal or coke
Buckles, 1 inch or less in greatest dimension.
Burlap
Buttons.
Cards, playing.
Cellophane and celluloid in sheets, bands, or strips
Chemicals, drugs, medicinals, and similar substances, when imported in capsules, pills, tablets, lozenges, or troches
Cigars and cigarettes.
Covers, straw bottle.
Dies, diamond wire, unmounted
Dowels, wooden.
Effects, theatrical
Eggs.
Feathers
Firewood
Flooring, not further manufactured than planed, tongued and grooved.
Flowers, artificial, except bunches.
Flowers, cut.
Glass, cut to shape and size for use in clocks, hand, pocket, and purse mirrors, and other glass of similar shapes and size, not including lenses or watch crystals.
Glides, furniture, except glides with prongs.
Hairnets.
Hides, raw.
Hooks, fish (except snelled fish hooks).
Hoops (wood), barrel
Lathes.
Leather, except finished.
Livestock
Lumber, except finished.
Lumber, sawed.
Metal bars except concrete reinforcement bars, billets, blocks, blooms, ingots, pigs, plates, sheets, except galvanized sheets, shafting, slabs, and metal in similar forms

Mica not further manufactured than cut or stamped to dimension, shape, or form
Monuments
Nails, spikes, and staples
Natural products, such as vegetables, fruit, nuts, berries, and live or dead animals, fish and birds, all the foregoing which are in their natural state or not advanced in any manner further than is necessary for their safe transportation.
Nets, bottle wire.
Paper, newsprint
Paper, stencil.
Paper, stock
Parchment and vellum.
Parts, for machines imported from same country as parts.
Pickets (wood).
Pins, tuning.
Plants, shrubs, and other nursery stock.
Plugs, tie.
Poles, bamboo
Posts (wood), fence
Pulpwood.
Rags (including wiping rags).
Rails, joint bars, and tie plates of steel.
Ribbon.
Rivets.
Rope, including wire rope, cordage, cords, twines, threads, and yarns.
Scrap and waste
Screws.
Shims, track
Shingles (wood), bundles of, except bundles of red-cedar shingles.
Skins, fur, dressed or dyed.
Skins, raw fur
Sponges.
Springs, watch.
Stamps, postage and revenue, and government-stamped envelopes and postal cards bearing no printing other than the official imprint thereon.
Staves (wood), barrel.
Steel, hoop
Sugar, maple
Ties (wood), railroad.
Tiles, not over 1 inch in greatest dimension.
Timbers, sawed.
Tips, penholder.
Trees, Christmas.
Weights, analytical and precision, in sets
Wicking, candle
Wire, except barbed.

Unless an article being shipped to the United States is specifically named in the foregoing list, it would be advisable for an exporter to obtain advice from U.S. Customs before concluding that it is exempted from marking. If articles on the foregoing list are repacked in the United States, the new packages must be labeled to indicate the country of origin of the articles contained therein. Importers must certify on entry that, if they repackage, they will properly mark the repackaged containers; if they do not package, but resell to repackagers, notification of the marking requirements will be given to such repackagers. Failure to comply with the certification requirements may subject importers to penalties and marking duties.

OTHER EXCEPTIONS

The following classes of articles are also excepted from marking to indicate the country of their origin. (The usual container in which one of these articles is imported will also be excepted from marking.):

- An article imported for use by the importer and not intended for sale in its imported or any other form.

- An article which is to be processed in the United States by the importer or for his account otherwise than for the purpose of concealing the origin of the article and in such manner that any mark of origin would necessarily be obliterated, destroyed, or permanently concealed.

- An article with respect to which an ultimate purchaser in the United States, by reason of the character of the article, or by reason of the circumstances of its importation, must necessarily know the country of origin even though the article is not marked to indicate its origin. The clearest application of this exemption is when the contract between the ultimate purchaser in the United States and the supplier abroad insures that the order will be filled only with articles grown, manufactured, or produced in a named country.

The following classes of articles are also excepted from marking to indicate the country of their origin:

- Articles that are incapable of being marked.

- Articles that cannot be marked prior to shipment to the United States without injury.

- Articles that cannot be marked prior to shipment to the United States, except at an expense economically prohibitive of their importation.

- Articles for which the marking of the containers will reasonably indicate the origin of the articles.

- Crude substances.

- Articles produced more than 20 years prior to their importation into the United States.

- Articles entered or withdrawn from warehouse for immediate exportation or for transportation and exportation.

Although such articles are exempted from marking to indicate their country of origin, the outermost containers in which the articles will ordinarily reach the ultimate purchaser in the United States must be marked to show the country of origin of such articles.

When marking the article's container will reasonably indicate the article's country of origin, the article itself may be exempt from such marking. This exemption applies only when the articles will reach the ultimate purchaser in an unopened container. For example, articles which reach the retail purchaser in sealed containers marked clearly to indicate the country of origin come within this exception. Materials to be used in building or manufacture by the builder or manufacturer who will receive the materials in unopened cases likewise come within the exemption. The following articles, as well as their containers, are excepted from marking to indicate the country of their origin:

- Products of American fisheries that are free of duty.

- Products of possessions of the United States.

- Products of the United States exported and returned.

- Articles valued at not more than $5 that are passed without entry.

Special country-of-origin marking rules for goods of a NAFTA country are addressed in Customs publication No. 571, *NAFTA: A Guide to Customs Procedures.*

30. SPECIAL MARKING REQUIREMENTS

The country of origin marking requirements are separate and apart from any special marking or labeling required on specific products by other agencies. It is recommended that the specific agency be contacted for any special marking or labeling requirements.

Certain articles are subject to special country of origin marking requirements: Iron and steel pipe and pipe fittings; manhole rings, frames, or covers; and compressed gas cylinders must generally be marked by one of four methods: die-stamped, cast-in-mold lettering, etching (acid or electrolytic) or engraving. In addition, none of the exceptions from marking discussed above are applicable to iron and steel pipe and pipe fittings.

The following articles and parts thereof shall be marked legibly and conspicuously to indicate their origin by die-stamping, cast-in-the-mold lettering, etching (acid or electrolytic), engraving, or by means of metal plates that bear the prescribed marking and that are securely attached to the article in a conspicuous place by welding, screws, or rivets:

Knives, clippers, shears, safety razors, surgical instruments, scientific and laboratory instruments, pliers, pincers and vacuum containers.

Watch movements are required to be marked on one or more of the bridges or top plates to show (1) the name of the country of manufacture, (2) the name of the manufacturer or purchaser, and (3) in words, the number of jewels, if any, serving a mechanical purpose as frictional bearings.

Clock movements shall be marked on the most visible part of the front or back plate to show (1) the name of the country of manufacture, (2) the name of the manufacturer or purchaser, and (3) the number of jewels, if any.

Watch cases shall be marked on the inside or outside of the back cover to show (1) the name of the country of manufacture, and (2) the name of the manufacturer or purchaser.

Clock cases and other cases provided for in Chapter 91, HTSUS, are required to be marked on the most visible part of the outside of the back to show the name of the country of manufacture.

The terms "watch movement" and "clock movement" refer to devices regulated by a balance wheel and hairspring, quartz crystal, or any other system capable of determining intervals of time, with a display or system to which a mechanical display can be incorporated. "Watch movements" include devices that do not exceed 12 mm in thickness and 50 mm in width, length, or diameter; "clock movements" include devices that do not meet the watch movement dimensional specifications. The term "cases" includes inner and outer cases, containers, and housings for movements, together with parts or pieces, such as, but not limited to, rings, feet, posts, bases, and outer frames, and any auxiliary or incidental features, which (with appropriate movements) serve to complete the watches, clocks, time switches, and other apparatus provided for in Chapter 91, HTSUS.

Articles required to be marked in accordance with the special marking requirements in Chapter 91 must be conspicuously and indelibly marked by cutting, die-sinking, engraving, or stamping. Articles required to be so marked shall be denied entry unless marked in exact conformity with these requirements.

Movements with optoelectronic display only and cases designed for use therewith, whether entered as separate articles or as components of assembled watches or clocks, are not subject to the special marking requirements. These items need only be marked with the marking requirements of 19 USC 1304.

Parts of any of the foregoing not including those above mentioned.

In addition to the special marking requirements set forth above, all watches of foreign origin must comply with the usual country of origin marking requirements. Customs considers the country of origin of watches to be the country of manufacture of the watch movement. The name of this country should appear either on the outside back cover or on the face of the dial.

31. MARKING—FALSE IMPRESSION

Section 42 of the Trade-Mark Act of 1946 (15 U.S.C. 1124) provides, among other things, that no imported article of foreign origin which bears a name or mark calculated to induce the public to believe that it was manufactured in the United States, or in any foreign country or locality other than the country or locality in which it was actually manufactured, shall be admitted to entry at any customs house in the United States.

In many cases, the words "United States," the letters "U.S.A.," or the name of any city or locality in the United States appearing on an imported article of foreign origin, or on the containers thereof, are considered to be calculated to induce the public to believe that the article was manufactured in the United States unless the name of the country of origin appears in close proximity to the name which indicates a domestic origin. Merchandise discovered after conditional release to have been missing a required country of origin marking may be ordered redelivered to Customs custody. If such delivery is not promptly made, liquidated damages may be assessed against the Customs bond.

(See 19 CFR 141.113(a); cf., 19 CFR Part 172 and Customs Form 4647.)

An imported article bearing a name or mark prohibited by Section 42 of the Trade-Mark Act is subject to seizure and forfeiture. However, upon the filing of a petition by the importer prior to final disposition of the article, the port director of Customs may release it upon the condition that the prohibited marking be removed or obliterated or that the article and containers be properly marked; or the port director may permit the article to be exported or destroyed under Customs supervision and without expense to the government.

Section 43 of the Trade-Mark Act of 1946 (15 U.S.C. 1125) prohibits the entry of goods marked or labeled with a false designation of origin or with any false description or representation, including words or other symbols tending to falsely describe or represent the same. Deliberate removal, obliteration, covering, or altering of required country of origin markings after release from Customs custody is also a crime punishable by fines and imprisonment (19 U.S.C. 1304(i)).

32. USER FEES

Customs user fees were established by the Consolidated Omnibus Budget Reconciliation Act of 1985. This legislation was expanded in 1986 to include a merchandise processing fee. Also in 1986, Congress enacted the Water Resources Development Act, which authorized the Customs Service to collect a harbor maintenance fee for the Army Corps of Engineers. Further legislation has extended the User Fee Program until 2003.

The merchandise processing fee (MPF) is 0.21 percent ad valorem on formally-entered imported merchandise (generally entries valued over $2,000), subject to a minimum fee of $25 per entry and a maximum fee of $485 per entry. On informal entries (those valued at less than $2,000), the MPFs are: $2 for automated entries, $6 for manual entries not prepared by Customs, and $9 for manual entries that are prepared by Customs.

The following changes in the MPF are effective for entries submitted on or after January 1, 1994:

- Goods imported directly from Canada that qualify under NAFTA for marking as goods of Canadian orgin are not assessed the MPF. This applies to all MPF fees: formal, informal, manually prepared, or automated.

- The formula previously used to prorate mixed Canadian/non-Canadian goods is discontinued. All entries containing any goods which do not qualify under NAFTA will be assessed the appropriate MPF.

There is no immediate change to the MPF assessed on goods of Mexican origin. However, effective June 30, 1999, the MPF will cease to exist for goods which qualify to be marked as goods of Mexico under NAFTA.

The harbor maintenance fee is an ad valorem fee assessed on port use associated with imports, admissions into foreign trades zones, domestic shipments, and passenger transportations. The fee is assessed only at ports that benefit from the expenditure of funds by the Army Corps of Engineers for maintaining and improving the port trade zones. The fee is 0.125 percent of the value of the cargo and is paid quarterly, except for imports, which are paid at the time of entry. Customs deposits the harbor maintenance fee collections into the Harbor Maintenance Trust Fund. The funds are made available, subject to appropriation, to the Army Corps of Engineers for the improvement and maintenance of United States ports and harbors.

SPECIAL REQUIREMENTS

33. PROHIBITIONS, RESTRICTIONS, OTHER AGENCY REQUIREMENTS

The importation of certain classes of merchandise may be prohibited or restricted to protect the economy and security of the United States, to safeguard consumer health and well-being, and to preserve domestic plant and animal life. Some commodities are also subject to an import quota or a restraint under bilateral trade agreements and arrangements.

Many of these prohibitions and restrictions on importations are subject, in addition to Customs requirements, to the laws and regulations administered by other United States government agencies with which Customs cooperates in enforcement. These laws and regulations may, for example, prohibit entry; limit entry to certain ports; restrict routing, storage, or use; or require treatment, labeling, or processing as a condition of release. Customs clearance is given only if these various additional requirements are met. This applies to all types of importations, including those made by mail and those placed in foreign trade zones.

The foreign exporter should make certain that the United States importer has provided proper information to (1) permit the submission of necessary information concerning packing, labeling, etc., and (2) that necessary arrangements have been made by the importer for entry of the merchandise into the United States.

It may be impracticable to list all articles specifically; however, various classes of articles are discussed in this chapter. Foreign exporters and U.S. importers should consult the agency mentioned for detailed information and guidance, as well as for any changes to the laws and regulations under which the commodities are controlled. Addresses, phone numbers, and Web sites for these agencies are listed in the appendix.

AGRICULTURAL COMMODITIES

1. Cheese, Milk, and Dairy Products. Cheese and cheese products are subject to requirements of the Food and Drug Administration and the Department of Agriculture. Most importations of cheese require an import license and are subject to quotas administered by the Department of Agriculture, Foreign Agricultural Service, Washington, DC 20250 (see Chapter 36).

The importation of milk and cream is subject to requirements of the Food, Drug and Cosmetic Act and the Import Milk Act. These products may be imported only by holders of permits from the Department of Health and Human Services, Food and Drug Administration, Center for Food Safety and Applied Nutrition, Office of Food Labeling (HFS-156), 200 "C" Street NW, Washington, DC 20204; and the Department of Agriculture.

2. Fruits, Vegetables, and Nuts. Certain agricultural commodities (including fresh tomatoes, avocados, mangoes, limes, oranges, grapefruit, green peppers, Irish potatoes, cucumbers, eggplants, dry onions, walnuts and filberts, processed dates, prunes, raisins, and olives in tins) must meet United States import requirements relating to grade, size, quality, and maturity (7 U.S.C. 608(e)). These commodities are inspected and an inspection certificate must be issued by the Food Safety and Inspection Service of the Department of Agriculture to indicate import compliance. Inquiries on general requirements should be made to the Agricultural Marketing Service of the Department of Agriculture, Washington, DC 20250. Additional restrictions may be imposed by the Animal and Plant Health Inspection Service of that department, Washington, DC 20782, under the

Plant Quarantine Act, and by the Food and Drug Administration, Division of Import Operations and Policy (HFC-170), 5600 Fishers Lane, Rockville, MD 20857, under the Federal Food, Drug and Cosmetic Act.

3. Insects. Insects in a live state which are injurious to cultivated crops (including vegetables, field crops, bush fruit, and orchard, forest, or shade trees) and the eggs, pupae, or larvae of such insects are prohibited importation, except for scientific purposes, under regulations prescribed by the Secretary of Agriculture.

All packages containing live insects or their eggs, pupae, or larvae, which are not injurious to crops or trees, are permitted entry into the United States only if covered by a permit issued by the Animal and Plant Health Inspection Service of the Department of Agriculture and are not prohibited by the U.S. Fish and Wildlife Service.

4. Livestock and Animals. Inspection and quarantine requirements of the Animal and Plant Health Inspection Service (APHIS) must be met for the importation of (1) all cloven-hoofed animals (ruminants), such as cattle, sheep, deer, antelope, camels, giraffes; (2) swine including the various varieties of wild hogs and the meat from such animals; (3) horses, asses, mules, and zebras; (4) animal by-products, such as untanned hides, wool, hair, bones, bone meal, blood meal, animal casings, glands, organs, extracts, or secretions of ruminants and swine (if animal by-product for food, drug, or cosmetic, it is also regulated by the Food and Drug Administration); (5) animal germ-plasm, including embryos and semen; and (6) hay and straw. A permit for importation must be obtained from APHIS before shipping from the country of origin.

In addition, all animal imports must be accompanied by a health certificate. Entry procedures for livestock and animals from Mexico and Canada are not as rigorous as those for animals from other countries. Entry of animals is restricted to certain ports which are designated as quarantine stations. A special offshore, high-security facility, the Harry S. Truman Animal Import Center, has been established at Key West, Florida, so that livestock can be safely quarantined when imported from countries affected with foot-and-mouth disease or other serious animal diseases that do not occur in the United States. All nondomesticated animals must meet the requirements of the Fish and Wildlife Service.

5. Meat and Meat Products. All commercial shipments of meat and meat food products (derived from cattle, sheep, swine, goats, and horses) offered for entry into the United States are subject to the regulations of the Department of Agriculture and must be inspected by the Animal and Plant Health Inspection Service (APHIS) and the Food Safety and Inspection Service of that department prior to release by U.S. Customs. Meat products from other sources (including, but not limited to wild game) are subject to APHIS regulations; the provisions of the Federal Food, Drug, and Cosmetics Act, enforced by the Food and Drug Administration; and the U.S. Fish and Wildlife Service.

6. Plant and Plant Products. The importation of plants and plant products is subject to regulations of the Department of Agriculture and may be restricted or prohibited. Plants and plant products include fruits, vegetables, plants, nursery stock, bulbs, roots, seeds, certain fibers including cotton and broomcorn, cut flowers, sugarcane, certain cereals, elm logs and elm lumber with bark attached. Import permits are required. Further information should be obtained from the Animal and Plant Heath Inspection Service. Also, certain endangered species of plants may be prohibited or require permits or certificates. The Food and Drug Administration also regulates plant and plant products, particularly fruits and vegetables.

7. Poultry and Poultry Products. Poultry, live, dressed, or canned; eggs, including eggs for hatching; and egg products are subject to the requirements and regulations of the Animal and Plant Heath Inspection Service and the Food Safety and Inspection Service of the Department of Agriculture.

Except for live poultry and poultry products entering through land ports from Canada, permits are required, as well as special marking and labeling; and in some cases, foreign inspection certification. The term "poultry" is defined as any live or slaughtered domesticated bird, e.g., chickens, turkeys, ducks, geese, swans, partridges, guinea fowl, pea fowl, non-migratory ducks, pigeons, and doves. Other birds (e.g., commercial, domestic, or pen-raised grouse, pheasants and quail, and migratory birds) as well as certain egg products are subject to APHIS regulations and to the provisions of the Federal Food, Drug, and Cosmetics Act, enforced by the Food and Drug Administration. Inquiry should also be made to the Fish and Wildlife Service, Washington, DC 20240, about their requirements, restrictions, and prohibitions.

8. Seeds. The importation into the United States of agricultural and vegetable seeds and screenings is governed by the provisions of the Federal Seed Act of 1939 and regulations of the Agricultural Marketing Service, Department of Agriculture. Shipments are detained pending the drawing and testing of samples.

ARMS, AMMUNITION, AND RADIOACTIVE MATERIALS

9. Arms, Ammunition, Explosives, and Implements of War. These items are prohibited importations except when a license is issued by the Bureau of Alcohol, Tobacco and Firearms of the Department of the Treasury, Washington, DC 20226, (202) 927-8320, or the importation is in compliance with the regulations of that department. The temporary importation, in-transit movement, and exportation of arms and ammunition is prohibited unless a license is issued by the Office of Defense Trade Controls, Department of State, Washington, DC 20520, or unless a license exemption is available as set forth in 22 CFR 123.4 and other sections of 22 CFR. Any questions about exporting shotguns should be referred to the U.S. Department of Commerce, Exporter Assistance Staff, Washington, DC 20230.

10. Radioactive Materials and Nuclear Reactors. Many radioisotopes, all forms of uranium, thorium, and plutonium, and all nuclear reactors imported into the United States are subject to the regulations of the Nuclear Regulatory Commission in addition to import regulations imposed by any other agency of the United States. Authority to import these commodities

or articles containing these commodities requires a license from the Nuclear Regulatory Commission, Washington, DC 20555. (Refer to 10 CFR Part 110.)

Radioisotopes and radioactive sources intended for medical use are subject to the provisions of the Federal Food, Drug, and Cosmetic Act, enforced by the Food and Drug Administration.

In order to comply with the Nuclear Regulatory Commission requirements, the importer must be aware of the identity and amount of any NRC-controlled radioisotopes, or uranium, thorium, and plutonium, and of any nuclear reactor being imported into the United States. To assure passage through Customs, the importer must demonstrate to U.S. Customs which Nuclear Regulatory Commission authority the controlled commodity is being imported under. The authority cited may be the number of a specific or general license, or the specific section of the Nuclear Regulatory Commission regulations which establishes a general license or grants an exemption to the regulations. The foreign exporter may save time for the prospective importer by furnishing the importer with complete information concerning the presence of NRC-controlled commodities in U.S. importation.

CONSUMER PRODUCTS— ENERGY CONSERVATION

11. Household appliances. The Energy Policy and Conservation Act, as amended, calls for energy standards for certain major household appliances and for labeling them to indicate expected energy consumption or efficiency. The Department of Energy, Office of Codes and Standards, Washington, DC 20585, is responsible for test procedures and energy performance standards. The Federal Trade Commission, Division of Enforcement, Washington, DC 20580, regulates the labeling of these appliances. The Act covers the following household appliances: (1) refrigerators, refrigerator-freezers and freezers; (2) room air conditioners; (3) central air conditioners and central air-conditioning heat pumps; (4) water heaters; (5) furnaces; (6) dishwashers; (7) clothes washers; (8) clothes dryers; (9) direct heating equipment; (10) kitchen ranges and ovens; (11) pool heaters; and (12) flourescent lamp ballasts.

12. Commercial and industrial equipment. The Energy Policy Act of 1992 (EPACT) calls for energy performance standards for certain commercial and industrial equipment. The Department of Energy, Office of Codes and Standards, Washington, DC 20585, is responsible for test procedures and energy performance standards. The EPACT covers the following equipment: (1) small and large commercial-package air-conditioning and heating equipment; (2) packaged terminal air conditioners and heat pumps; (3) warm-air furnaces; (4) packaged boilers; (5) storage water heaters; (6) instantaneous water heaters; (7) unfired hot-water storage tanks; (8) large electric motors (one to 200 horsepower) whether shipped separately or as a part of a larger assembly; (9) 4-foot medium bi-pin, 2-foot U-shaped, 8-foot slimline, and 8-foot high-output flourescent lamps; and (10) incandescent reflector lamps. In addition, the EPACT calls for water conservation standards for the following plumbing products: (1) lavatory faucets; (2) lavatory replacement aerators; (3) kitchen faucets; (4) kitchen replacement faucets; (5) metering faucets; (6) gravity tank-type toilets; (7) flushometer tank toilets; (8) electromechanical hydraulic toilets; (9) blowout toilets; and (10) urinals.

Importation of these products must comply with the applicable Department of Energy and Federal Trade Commission requirements. Importers should contact these agencies for requirements which will be in effect at the time of anticipated shipment. It should be noted that not all appliances are covered by requirements of both agencies.

CONSUMER PRODUCTS—SAFETY

Any consumer product offered for importation will be refused admission if the product fails to comply with an applicable product safety standard or regulation or with a specified labeling or certification requirement or is determined to present a substantial product hazard. These requirements are administered by the U.S. Consumer Product Safety Commission (CPSC), Washington, DC 20207.

13. Toys and Children's Articles. Toys and other children's articles cannot be imported into the United States if they fail to comply with applicable regulations issued under the Federal Hazardous Substances Act. The major regulations dealing with toys are described below. Toys or other articles intended for children under three cannot have small parts that present choking hazards to small children. The Child Safety Protection Act (an amendment to the Federal Hazardous Substances Act) and its implementing regulations require warning labeling on toys for children who are at least three years of age, but less than six years of age, and that present choking hazards from small parts. These regulations also cover balloons, small balls (small balls for children under age three are banned), and marbles. Electric toys, rattles, pacifiers, and cribs are also subject to specific safety regulations. CPSC's regulations contain tests used to define hazardous sharp edges and points on toys and other children's articles. Lawn darts are banned.

14. Lead In Paint. Paint and other similar surface coating materials intended for consumer use are banned if they contain more than 0.06 percent lead. This ban also applies to furniture with paint that exceeds 0.06 percent lead and to toys or other articles intended for use by children with paint that exceeds 0.06 percent lead. Such products cannot be admitted into the United States. Although this ban applies to "surface coatings," CPSC can take action, under the Federal Hazardous Substances Act, against other lead-containing products if the lead content results in a substantial risk of injury or illness.

15. Bicycles and Bicycle Helmets. Bicycles cannot be admitted unless they meet regulations issued under the Federal Hazardous Substances Act. The CPSC also has mandatory safety standards for bicycle helmets. Bicycle helmets imported after March 10, 1999, will not be admitted unless they meet CPSC's final Safety Standard for Bicycle Helmets. At that time, bicycle helmets will need to be accompanied by a Certificate of Compliance. Bicycle helmets currently imported must meet one of several interim standards.

16. Fireworks. The fireworks regulations issued under the Federal Hazardous Substance Act set labeling requirements and technical specifications for consumer fireworks. Large fireworks, such as cherry bombs and M-80s, are banned for consumer use. Large reloadable mortar shell fireworks are banned, and large multiple-tube mine and shell fireworks are subject to specific requirements to prevent tip-over. Fireworks not meeting any of these requirements cannot be imported into the United States.

17. Flammable Fabrics. Any article of wearing apparel, fabric or interior furnishing cannot be imported into the United States if it fails to conform to an applicable flammability standard issued under the Flammable Fabrics Act. These flammability standards cover general wearing apparel, children's sleepwear, mattresses (including futons), and carpets and rugs. Certain products can be imported into the United States, as provided in Section 11(c) of the Act, for the purpose of finishing or processing to render such products not so highly flammable as to be dangerous when worn by individuals, provided that the exporter states on the invoice or other paper relating to the shipment that the shipment is being made for that purpose.

18. Art Materials. Art materials cannot be imported into the United States unless they meet the Labeling of Hazardous Art Materials Act (LHAMA) of 1988, which is an amendment to the Federal Hazardous Substances Act. LHAMA requires that chronically hazardous art materials carry the warning labeling specified in an industry standard, ASTM D-4236. This standard also requires that art materials carry a label certifying that they have been reviewed by a toxicologist and identifying any known hazards.

19. Cigarette Lighters. Disposable and novelty cigarette lighters cannot be admitted into the United States unless they meet a safety standard issued under the Consumer Product Safety Act that requires that they be child resistant. All nonrefillable lighters, and refillable lighters whose customs value is less than $2.00 and that use gas as a fuel, are considered to be "disposable lighters" and are covered by the standard. Novelty lighters are lighters (using any type of fuel) which have entertaining audio or visual effects or that depict articles commonly recognized as intended for use by children under five

years of age. Manufacturers must test lighters, keep records and report the results to CPSC. A Certificate of Compliance must accompany each shipping unit of the product, or otherwise be furnished to the distributor or retailer to whom the product is delivered by the manufacturer, private labeler or importer.

20. Other Regulations and Standards. CPSC has issued a number of other safety standards and regulations. These have generally been of less interest to the importing community because fewer of these items are imported. These include:

- Architectural glazing,
- Matchbooks,
- CB and TV antennas,
- Walk-behind power lawn mowers,
- Swimming pool slides,
- Cellulose insulation,
- Garage door operators,
- Unstable refuse bins,
- Flammable contact adhesives,
- Patching compounds with asbestos,
- Emberizing materials with asbestos,
- Household chemicals,
- Refrigerator doors,
- Poison Prevention Packaging Act (requires child-resistant packaging of certain drugs and household chemicals).

ELECTRONIC PRODUCTS

21. Radiation-Producing Products, Including Sonic Radiation. Television products that incorporate a cathode ray tube, cold-cathode gas discharge tubes, microwave ovens, cabinet and diagnostic X-ray equipment, laser products, ultrasound physical therapy equipment, sunlamps, CD–ROMs, cellular and cordless telephones, and other electronic products for which there are radiation performance standards, are subject to the Federal Food, Drug, and Cosmetic Act, Chapter V, Subchapter C—Electronic Product Radiation (formerly called the Radiation Control Health and Safety Act of 1968). An electronic product (a) for which there is a radiation performance standard *and* (b) that is imported for sale or use in the United States may be imported only if a declaration (Form FDA 2877) is filed with each importer's entry notice. Form FDA 2877 is available from the Food and Drug Administration, Center for Devices and Radiological Health, Rockville, MD 20850.

The declaration must describe the compliance status of the product. The importer must affirm that the product was (1) not subject to a standard (e.g., manufactured prior to the effective date of the applicable federal standard), or (2) complies with the standard and has a label affixed by the manufacturer certifying compliance, or (3) does not comply with the standard but is being imported only for purposes of research, investigation, study, demonstration, or training, or (4) does not now comply with the standard but will be brought into compliance. The provisions of the Federal Food, Drug, and Cosmetic Act, Chapter V, Subchapter C — Electronic Product Radiation — apply to electronic products manufactured in the United States as well as to imported products.

22. Radio Frequency Devices. Radios, tape recorders, stereos, televisions, citizen band radios or combinations thereof, and other radio frequency devices are subject to radio emission standards of the Federal Communications Commission, Washington, DC 20554, under the Communications Act of 1934, as amended. Importations of such products may be accompanied by an FCC declaration (FCC 740) certifying that the imported model or device is in conformity with, will be brought into conformity, or is exempt from, the Federal Communication Commission requirements.

FOODS, DRUGS, COSMETICS, AND MEDICAL DEVICES

23. Foods, Cosmetics, Etc. The importation into the United States of food, drugs, devices, and cosmetics is governed by the provisions of the Federal Food, Drug, and Cosmetic Act, which is administered by the Food and Drug Administration of the Department of Health and Human Services, Rockville, MD 20857. That Act prohibits the importation of articles that are adulterated or misbranded, including products that are defective, unsafe, filthy, or produced under unsanitary conditions. The term "misbranded" includes statements, designs, or pictures in labeling that are false or misleading, or that fail to provide required information in labeling. The Act also prohibits the importation of pharmaceuticals that have not been approved by the FDA for admission into the United States.

Imported products regulated by the Food and Drug Administration are subject to inspection at the time of entry. Shipments found not to comply with the laws and regulations are subject to refusal. They must be brought into compliance, destroyed, or re-exported. At the discretion of the Food and Drug Administration, an importer may be permitted to bring a nonconforming importation into compliance if it is possible to do so. Any sorting, reprocessing, or relabeling must be supervised by the Food and Drug Administration at the importer's expense.

Various imported foods such as confectionery, dairy products, poultry, eggs and egg products, meats, fruits, nuts, and vegetables are also subject to requirements of other agencies as discussed in this book. Certain aquatic species may also be subject to the requirements of the National Marine Fisheries Service of the National Oceanic and Atmosphere Administration of the Department of Commerce, 1335 East-West Highway, Silver Spring, MD 20910.

24. Biological Drugs. The manufacture and importation of biological products for human consumption are regulated under the Public Health Service Act. Domestic and foreign manufacturers of such products must obtain a U.S. license for both the manufacturing establishment and the product intended to be produced or imported. Additional information may be obtained from the Food and Drug Administration, Department of Health and Human Services, Rockville, MD 20857.

Biological drugs for animals are regulated under the Virus Serum Toxin Act administered by the Department of Agriculture. The importation of viruses, serums, toxins and analogous products, and organisms and vectors for use in the treatment of domestic animals, is prohibited unless the importer holds a permit from the Department of Agriculture covering the specific product. These importations are also subject to special labeling requirements.

25. Biological Materials and Vectors. The importation into the United States for sale, barter, or exchange of any virus, therapeutic serum, toxin, antitoxin, or analogous products, or arsphenamine or its derivatives (or any other trivalent organic arsenic compound), except materials to be used in research experiments, applicable to the prevention, treatment, or cure of diseases or injuries of man is prohibited unless these products have been propagated or prepared at any establishment holding an unsuspended and unrevoked U.S. license for such manufacturing issued by the Secretary, Department of Health and Human Services. Samples of the U.S.-licensed product must accompany each importation for forwarding by the port director of Customs at the port of entry to the Director, Center for Biologics Evaluation and Research, 1401 Rockville Pike, Bethesda, MD 20852.

A permit from the U.S. Public Health Service, Centers for Disease Control and Prevention, Atlanta, GA 30333, is required for shipments of any etiological agent or insect, animal or plant vector of human disease or any exotic living insect, animal, or plant capable of being a vector of human disease.

26. Narcotic Drugs and Derivatives. The importation of controlled substances including narcotics, marijuana and other dangerous drugs, is prohibited except when imported in compliance with regulations of the Drug Enforcement Administration of the Department of Justice, Arlington, VA 22202. Examples of some of the prohibited controlled substances are amphetamines; barbiturates; coca leaves and derivatives such as cocaine; hallucinogenic substances such as LSD, mescaline, peyote, marijuana and other forms of cannabis; opiates, including methadone; opium, including opium derivatives such as morphine and heroin; synthetic substitutes for narcotic drugs, and anabolic steroids.

27. Drug Paraphernalia. Items of drug paraphernalia are prohibited from importation or exportation under Section 863, Title 21 of the United States Code. The term "drug paraphernalia" means any equipment, product, or material

of any kind which is primarily intended or designed for use in manufacturing, compounding, converting, concealing, producing, processing, preparing, injecting, ingesting, inhaling, or otherwise introducing into the human body a controlled substance, possession of which is unlawful under the Controlled Substances Act (Title II of Public Law 91-513). Items of drug paraphernalia include, but are not limited to, the following items:

- Metal, wooden, acrylic, glass, stone, plastic, or ceramic pipes with or without screens, permanent screens, hashish heads, or punctured metal bowls;
- Water pipes;
- Carburetion tubes and devices;
- Smoking and carburetion masks;
- Roach clips; meaning objects used to hold burning material, such as a marijuana cigarette, that has become too small or too short to be held in the hand;
- Miniature spoons with level capacities of one-tenth cubic centimeter or less;
- Chamber pipes;
- Carburetor pipes;
- Electric pipes;
- Air-driven pipes;
- Chillums;
- Bongs;
- Ice pipes or chillers;
- Wired cigarette papers; or
- Cocaine freebase kits.

GOLD, SILVER, CURRENCY, AND STAMPS

28. Gold and Silver. The provisions of the National Stamping Act, as amended (15 U.S.C. 291-300) are enforced in part by U.S. Customs and by the FBI. Articles made of gold or alloys thereof are prohibited importation into the United States if the gold content is three one-thousandth parts below the indicated fineness. In the case of articles made of gold or gold alloy, including the solder and alloy of inferior fineness, three one-thousandth parts below the indicated fineness is permitted. Articles marked "sterling" or "sterling silver" must assay at least 0.925 of pure silver with a 0.004 divergence allowed. Other articles of silver or silver alloys must assay not less than 0.004 part below the indicated fineness thereof. Articles marked "coin" or "coin silver" must contain at least 0.900 part pure silver with an allowable divergence of 0.004 part below.

A person placing articles of gold or silver bearing a fineness or quality mark such as 14 K, sterling, etc., in the mail or in interstate commerce must place his name or registered trademark next to the fineness mark in letters the same size as the fineness mark. The trademark or name is not required at the time of importation; therefore, Customs has no direct responsibility for enforcement of the law. Persons making inquiry or seeking advice or interpretation of the law should consult the Department of Justice.

Articles bearing the words "United States Assay" are prohibited importations. Articles made wholly or in part of inferior metal and plated or filled with gold or silver or alloys thereof and which are marked with the degree of fineness must also be marked to indicate the plated or filled content, and in such cases, the use of the words "sterling" or "coin" is prohibited.

All restrictions on the purchase, holding, selling, or otherwise dealing with gold were removed effective December 31, 1974, and gold may be imported subject to the usual Customs entry requirements. Under the Hobby Protection Act, administered by the Bureau of Consumer Protection of the Federal Trade Commission, any imitation numismatic item must be plainly and permanently marked "copy"; those that do not comply are subject to seizure and forfeiture. Unofficial gold coin restrikes must be marked with the country of origin. It is advisable to obtain a copy of the legal proclamation under which the coins are issued, or else an affidavit of government sanction of coins should be secured from a responsible banking official if the proclamation is unavailable.

29. Counterfeit Articles. Articles bearing facsimiles or replicas of coins or securities of the United States or of any foreign country cannot be imported. Counterfeits of coins in circulation in the United States; counterfeited, forged, or altered obligations or other securities of the United States or of any foreign government; plates, dies, or other apparatus which may be used in making any of the foregoing, are prohibited importations.

30. Monetary Instruments. Under the Currency and Foreign Transactions Reporting Act, 31 U.S.C. 5311 et seq., if a person knowingly transports, is about to transport, or has transported, more than $10,000 in monetary instruments at one time to, through or from the United States; or if a person receives more than $10,000 at one time from or through a place outside the United States, a report of the transportation (Customs Form 4790) must be filed with the U.S. Customs Service. Monetary instruments include U.S. or foreign coin, currency; traveler's checks in any form, personal and other checks, and money orders, either in bearer-negotiable form or endorsed without restriction; and securities or stocks in bearer form. A bank check or money order made payable to a named person but not endorsed, or which bears a restrictive endorsement, is not considered to be a "monetary instrument." The Department of the Treasury regulations governing the report of monetary instruments are set forth at 31 CFR part 103.

PESTICIDES, TOXIC, AND HAZARDOUS SUBSTANCES

31. Pesticides. The Federal Insecticide, Fungicide, and Rodenticide Act (FIFRA) as amended, 1988, provides the statutory authority governing the importation of pesticides and devices into the United States. Promulgated under Section 17(c) of this authority, the U.S. Customs Service regulations at 19 CFR Parts 12.112-.117 describe the procedures governing the importation of pesticides and devices. Among the requirements described in these regulations, importers must submit a Notice of Arrival that has been submitted for review and approved by the EPA prior to the importation. Pesticides must be registered in accordance with FIFRA Section 3 or they will be refused entry into the United States. Devices are not subject to product registration, but the labeling of both pesticides and devices must bear the producer establishment number registered with the EPA. In addition, pesticides and devices will be refused entry if they are identified as adulterated or misbranded, if they in any other way violate the provisions of FIFRA, or if they are otherwise injurious to health or the environment.

32. Toxic Substances. The Toxic Substances Control Act (TSCA), effective January 1, 1977, regulates the manufacturing, importation, processing, distribution in commerce, use or disposal of any chemical substances or mixtures that are broadly defined in Section 3 of TSCA. Section 3 specifies that certain substances are excluded from the definition of "chemical substance" based upon their use. These substances include, but are not limited to, foods, drugs, cosmetics, and active ingredients in pesticides. Importations will not be released from Customs custody unless proper certification is presented to Customs that the import "complies with" or "is not subject to" the requirements of the Toxic Substances Control Act, or if it is already identified as a food, drug, or active pesticide ingredient. For further information from EPA, call the TSCA Assistance Information Service (202) 554-1404.

33. Hazardous Substances. The importation into the United States of dangerous, caustic or corrosive substances in packages suitable for household use and of hazardous substances is regulated by the Hazardous Substance Act; the Caustic Poison Act; the Food, Drug and Cosmetic Act; and the Consumer Product Safety Act. The marking, labeling, packaging, and transportation of hazardous materials, substances, wastes, and their containers is regulated by the Office of Hazardous Materials Transportation of the Department of Transportation, Washington, DC 20590. Hazardous waste is a special sub-category of hazardous substances and is regulated by the Resource Recovery and Conservation Act, which requires a special EPA manifest for both imports and exports.

TEXTILE, WOOL, AND FUR PRODUCTS

34. Textile Products. All textile fiber products imported into the United States shall be stamped, tagged, labeled, or otherwise marked with the following information as required by the Textile Fiber Products Identification Act, unless exempted from marking under Section 12 of the Act:

■ The generic names and percentages by weight of the constituent fibers present in the textile fiber product, exclusive of permissive ornamentation, in amounts of more than five percent, in order of predominance by weight, with any percentage of fiber or fibers required to be designated as "other fiber" or "other fibers" appearing last. Fibers present in amounts of five percent or less must be designated as "other fibers."

■ The name of the manufacturer or the name or registered identification number issued by the Federal Trade Commission of one or more persons marketing or handling the textile fiber product. A word trademark, used as a house mark, registered in the United States Patent Office, may be on labels in lieu of the name otherwise required, if the owner of such trademark furnishes a copy of the registration to the Federal Trade Commission prior to use.

■ The name of the country where processed or manufactured.

In order to enforce the Textile Fiber Products Identification Act, a commercial invoice covering a shipment of textile fiber products exceeding $500 in value and subject to the labeling requirements of the Act is required to show the information noted in Chapter 10, in addition to that ordinarily required on the invoices.

In addition to labeling requirements, the importation of textiles and textile products may, pursuant to Section 204 of the Agricultural Act of 1956, be subject to quota, visa or export-license requirements and additional entry requirements including declarations identifying the fabricated components.

Regulations and pamphlets containing the text of the Textile Fiber Products Identification Act may be obtained from the Federal Trade Commission, Washington, DC 20580.

35. Wool. Any product containing woolen fiber imported into the United States, with the exception of carpet, rugs, mats, upholsteries, and articles made more than 20 years prior to importation, shall be tagged, labeled, or otherwise clearly marked with the following information as required by the Wool Products Labeling Act of 1939:

- The percentage of the total fiber weight of the wool product, exclusive of ornamentation not exceeding five percent of the total fiber weight, of: (1) wool, (2) recycled wool, (3) each fiber other than wool if the percent by weight of such fiber is five percent or more, and (4) the aggregate of all other fibers.

- The maximum percent of the total weight of the wool product, of any nonfibrous loading, filling, or adulterating matter.

- The name of the manufacturer or person introducing the product in commerce in the United States; i.e., the importer. If the importer has a registered identification number issued by the Federal Trade Commission, that number may be used instead of the individual's name.

For the purpose of enforcing the Wool Products Labeling Act, a commercial invoice covering a shipment of wool products exceeding $500 in value and subject to the labeling requirements of the act is required to show the information noted in Chapter 10.

The provisions of the Wool Products Labeling Act apply to products manufactured in the United States as well as to imported products.

Pamphlets containing the text of the Wool Products Labeling Act and the regulations may be obtained from the Federal Trade Commission, Washington, DC 20580.

36. Fur. Any article of wearing apparel imported into the United States and made in whole or in part of fur or used fur, with the exception of articles made of new fur of which the cost or manufacturer's selling price does not exceed $7, shall be tagged, labeled, or otherwise clearly marked to show the following information as required by the Fur Products Labeling Act:

- The name of the manufacturer or person introducing the product in commerce in the United States; i.e., importer. If the

importer has a registered identification number, that number may be used instead of the individual's name.

- The name or names of the animal or animals that produced the fur as set forth in the Fur Products Name Guide and as determined under the rules and regulations.

- That the fur product contains used or damaged fur where such is the fact.

- That the fur product is bleached, dyed, or otherwise artificially colored when such is the fact.

- That the fur product is composed in whole or in substantial part of paws, tails, bellies, or waste fur when such is the fact.

- The name of the country of origin of any imported furs contained in a fur product.

For the purpose of enforcing the Fur Products Labeling Act, a commercial invoice covering a shipment of furs or fur products exceeding $500 in value is required to show the information noted in Chapter 10.

The provisions of the Fur Products Labeling Act apply to fur and fur products in the United States as well as to imported furs and fur products. Regulations and pamphlets containing the text of the Fur Products Labeling Act may be obtained from the Federal Trade Commission, Washington, DC 20580.

TRADEMARKS, TRADE NAMES, AND COPYRIGHTS

37. Trademarks and Trade Names. Articles bearing counterfeit trademarks are subject to seizure and forfeiture. A *counterfeit* trademark is defined as a spurious trademark that is identical with, or substantially indistinguishable from, a registered trademark. Marks that *copy or simulate* a registered trademark that has been recorded with Customs are subject to detention and possible seizure and forfeiture. The importation of "parallel" or "gray market" goods is restricted where the registered trademark has been recorded with Customs and gray-market protection has been afforded. In such instances, gray-market merchandise is subject to detention and possible seizure and forfeiture. The U.S. Customs Service also affords similar protection against unauthorized shipments bearing trade names that are recorded with Customs pursuant to regulations.

A personal exemption for merchandise bearing an infringing mark is provided for articles accompanying any person arriving in the United States when such articles are for his or her personal use and not for sale. Only one infringing item of each type bearing a registered trademark is permitted. An individual may take advantage of this exemption only once within a 30-day period (19 USC 1526 (d); 19 CFR 148.55).

38. Copyrights. Articles imported into the United States that are piratical of a registered copyright are subject to seizure and forfeiture.

WILDLIFE AND PETS

39. Wildlife and Pets. The importation of live wildlife (i.e., game animals, birds, plants) or any part or product made therefrom, and of birds' eggs, is subject to certain prohibitions, restrictions, permits and quarantine requirements of several government agencies. Imports or exports of wildlife, their parts or products must be declared at designated ports of the U.S. Fish and Wildlife Service, unless an exception is granted prior to the time of import or export. The Assistant Regional Director of Law Enforcement for the region in which the import or export will take place should be contacted for additional information or to request an exception to designated port permit.

Any commercial importer or exporter (with some exceptions) importing or exporting wildlife must obtain a license from the Fish and Wildlife Service. Applications and further information may be obtained from the Fish and Wildlife Service, Assistant Regional Director for Law Enforcement, for the region in which the importer or exporter is located.

Endangered species of wildlife and certain species of animals and birds are generally prohibited entry into the United States and may be imported or exported only under a permit granted by the U.S. Fish and Wildlife Service. Specific information concerning permit requirements should be obtained from the Fish and Wildlife Service, Office of Management Author-

ity, 4401 North Fairfax Drive, Arlington, VA 22203, or by calling 1-800-358-2104.

Antique articles (at least 100 years old) may be exempt from certain requirements of the U.S. Endangered Species Act. The Fish and Wildlife Service, Office of Management Authority, should be contacted for details.

The taking and importation of marine mammals and their products are subject to the requirements of the Marine Mammal Protection Act (MMPA) of 1972, as amended in 1994. The National Marine Fisheries Service (NMFS) and the Fish and Wildlife Service have jurisdiction under the MMPA for certain species and import activities. Additional requirements of the U.S. Endangered Species Act and the Convention on International Trade in Endangered Species (CITES) may apply. Prior to importing, both agencies should be contacted to learn the exact import requirements. Other NMFS import requirements may also apply for certain species covered by the International Commission for the Conservation of Atlantic Tunas, e.g., Atlantic bluefin tuna.

Certain mammals, birds, reptiles, amphibians, fish, snails, clams, insects, crustaceans, mollusks, other invertebrates and plants may be prohibited entry without the prior issuance of a permit either from the foreign wildlife authority or from the Fish and Wildlife Service, Office of Management Authority.

The importation into the United States of any wildlife, their parts or products is prohibited if the wildlife was captured, taken, shipped, or possessed contrary to the laws of the foreign country.

The importation of feathers or skins of any bird, except for scientific and educational purposes, is prohibited, except for the species noted in this paragraph. This prohibition does not apply to fully manufactured artificial flies used for fishing or to personally taken, noncommercial game birds. Feathers or skins of the following species are permitted entry: chickens, turkeys, guinea fowl, geese, ducks, pigeons, ostriches, rheas, English ring-necked pheasants, and pea fowl not taken from the wild.

On October 23, 1992, the Wild Bird Conservation Act became effective. This act focuses on live bird species listed in the Appendices to the Convention on International Trade in Endangered Species (CITES). Now, if you import live birds, you must meet the requirements of this law in addition to existing requirements of CITES, the Endangered Species Act, the Migratory Bird Treaty Act, or other applicable regulations. Import permits must be obtained from the Fish and Wildlife Service, Office of Management Authority.

Live birds, their parts and products that are protected under the Migratory Bird Treaty Act may be imported into the United States for scientific purposes or certain propagating purposes only under permits issued by the Fish and Wildlife Service, Office of Migratory Birds, located in the region where the importation will occur or where the importer resides.

Imports of birds (pets, migratory birds, falcons) are subject to the quarantine requirements of the USDA and Public Health Service. Quarantine space must be reserved in advance of import. Prior to export, health certificates must be obtained. Inquiries should be addressed to the appropriate agency.

On June 9, 1989, the U.S. Fish and Wildlife Service announced a ban on the importation of most African elephant ivory and any products made from it. The ban covers all commercial and noncommercial shipments, including personal baggage accompanying a tourist. There are limited exceptions for antiques, trophies, and personal household effects. For further information, contact the U.S. Fish and Wildlife Service, Office of Management Authority, 4401 N. Fairfax Drive, Arlington, VA 22203, Tel. 1-800-358-2104.

The importation of birds, cats, dogs, monkeys, and turtles is subject to the requirements of the U.S. Public Health Service, Centers for Disease Control, Quarantine Division, Atlanta, GA 30333; of the Veterinary Services of the Animal and Plant Health Inspection Service, Department of Agriculture, Hyattsville, MD 20782; and of the U.S. Fish and Wildlife Service. The importation of live turtles, tortoises, and terrapins with a carapace length of less than four inches, and the viable eggs of turtles, tor-

toises and terrapins, is allowed by the U.S. Public Health Service only under strict requirements as to purpose and quantity. The U.S. Public Heath Service does not allow the importation of live, non-human primates, including monkeys, as pets.

OTHER MISCELLANEOUS PROHIBITED OR RESTRICTED MERCHANDISE

White or yellow phosphorus matches, fireworks banned under federal or state restrictions, pepper shells, switchblade knives, and lottery tickets are prohibited.

40. Foreign Assets Control Restrictions. The Office of Foreign Assets Control administers regulations (31 CFR, Chapter V) which generally prohibit the importation of merchandise or goods that contain components from the following countries: Cuba, Iran, Iraq, Libya, North Korea, and Sudan. These restrictions apply to the country of origin, regardless of where the item was acquired. An Iranian rug acquired in England, for example, is still prohibited. Be aware, too, that origin can be conferred by entering the commerce of a sanctioned country: American-made jewelry acquired in Iran may be considered to be of Iranian origin if returned to the United States.

These proscriptions do not apply to informational materials such as pamphlets, books, tapes, films, or recordings, except those from Iraq.

Specific licenses are required to bring prohibited merchandise into the United States, but they are rarely granted. Foreign visitors to the United States, however, may usually be permitted to bring in small articles for personal use as accompanied baggage, depending upon the goods' country of origin.

Travelers should be aware of certain travel restrictions that may apply to these countries. Because of the strict enforcement of these prohibitions, those anticipating foreign travel to any of the countries listed above would do well to write in advance to the Office of Foreign Assets Control, Department of the Treasury, Washington, DC 20220, or to call (202) 622-2500.

41. Obscene, Immoral, Seditious Matter and Lottery Tickets. Section 305, Tariff Act of 1930, as amended, prohibits the importation of any book, writing, advertisement, circular, or picture containing any matter advocating or urging treason or insurrection against the United States, or forcible resistance to any law of the United States, or containing any threat to take the life of or inflict bodily harm upon any person in the United States; or any obscene book, writing, advertisement, circular, picture or other representation, figure, or image on or of paper or other material, or any instrument, or other article which is obscene or immoral, or any drug or medicine for causing unlawful abortion unless otherwise authorized by law (e.g., FDA-approved), or any lottery ticket (except if printed in Canada for use in a U.S.—or, in some cases, other foreign—lottery).

42. Petroleum and Petroleum Products. Importations of petroleum and petroleum products are subject to the requirements of the Department of Energy. An import license is no longer required, but an import authorization may be needed. These importations may be subject to an oil import license fee collected and administered by the Department of Energy. Inquiries should be directed to the Department of Energy, Washington, DC 20585.

43. Products of Convict or Forced Labor. Merchandise produced, mined, or manufactured, wholly or in part by means of the use of convict labor, forced labor, or indentured labor under penal sanctions is prohibited from importation, provided a finding has been published pursuant to section 12.42 of the Customs Regulations (19 CFR 12.42), that certain classes of merchandise from a particular country, produced by convict, forced, or indentured labor, were either being, or are likely to be, imported into the United States in violation of section 307 of the Tariff Act of 1930, as amended (19 U.S.C. 1307).

44. Unfair Competition. Section 337 of the Tariff Act, as amended, prohibits the importation of merchandise if the President finds that unfair methods of competition or unfair acts exist. This section is most commonly invoked in the case of patent violations, although a patent need not be at issue. Prohibition of entries of the merchandise in question generally is for the term of the patent, although a different term may be specified.

Following a section 337 investigation, the International Trade Commission may find that unfair methods of competition or unfair acts exist with respect to the importation of certain merchandise. After the International Trade Commission has issued an order, the President is allowed 60 days to take action to communicate his approval or disapproval of such determination. Should the 60 days expire without Presidential action, the order becomes final. During the 60-day period, or until the President acts, importation of the merchandise is allowed under a special bond, but it must be recalled by Customs if appropriate under the conditions of the order when it becomes final. If the President determines that entry of the merchandise is not in violation of section 337, the bond is canceled.

45. Importations of articles bearing the title, abbreviations, initials, symbols, emblems, seals, or badges of any subdivision of the Department of the Treasury, or likeness thereof, are prohibited unless the subdivision has authorized the use of the symbol, initials, etc. See 31 U.S.C. 333(c).

46. Artifacts/Cultural Property. A number of U.S. laws are applicable to importations of artifacts such as archaeological and ethnological objects. For example, U.S. law prohibits the importation of pre-Columbian monumental and architectural sculpture and murals from countries in Central and South America without proper export permits from the country of origin. U.S. Customs will not accept an export permit from a third country. Also, importations of certain archeological and ethnographic material from El Salvador, Guatemala, Peru, Mali, and Canada are specifically restricted from entering the United States unless they are accompanied by an export certificate issued by the country of origin. The U.S. Customs Service has published import restrictions on objects and artifacts of this nature in the Federal Register; these restrictions may also be viewed at the U.S. Information Agency's Web site, **www.usia.gov/education/culprop**. These restrictions are aimed at deterring the pillage of other countries' cultural heritage and at fostering opportunities for access to cultural objects for legitimate scientific, cultural, and educationsl purposes.

Federal law also prohibits the importation of any article of cultural property stolen from museums or from religious or secular public monuments. Importers should be aware that a treaty exists between the United States and Mexico on cultural property recovery. Would-be buyers of such property should be aware that, ulike purchases of customary tourist merchandise, purchases of cultural objects do not confer ownership should the object be found to be stolen. The U.S. National Stolen Property Act may be applicable in such cases, particularly if a country of origin declares by law that it owns all cultural objects, known or unknown, within its present-day political boundaries.

Purveyors of such merchandise have been known to offer fake export cerificates. Prospective buyers should be aware that Customs inspectors are expert at spotting fraudulent export certificates that accompany cultural property. Customs inspectors will also examine declaration forms to determine whether any false information has been entered, since this also constitutes a violation.

For current information about countries for which the United States has issued specific import restrictions, contact the United States Information Agency, Washington, DC (202) 619–6612, or visit the agency's Web site: **www.usia.gov/education/culprop**. For information about how these restrictions are enforced, contact the U.S. Customs Service Intellectual Property Rights Branch, (202) 927–2330.

34. ALCOHOLIC BEVERAGES

Any person or firm wishing to engage in the business of importing distilled spirits, wines, or malt beverages into the United States must first obtain an importer's basic permit from the Bureau of Alcohol, Tobacco and Firearms, Department of the Treasury, Washington, DC 20226, Tel. (202) 927-8110. That agency is responsible for administering the Federal Alcohol Administration Act.

Distilled spirits imported in bulk containers of a capacity of more than one gallon may be withdrawn from Customs custody only by persons to whom it is lawful to sell or otherwise dispose of distilled spirits in bulk. Bulk or bottled shipments of imported spirits or distilled or intoxicating liquors must, at the time of importation, be accompanied by a copy of a bill of lading or other documents such as an invoice, showing the name of the consignee, the nature of its contents, and the quantity contained therein (18 U.S.C. 1263).

U.S. Customs will not release alcoholic beverages destined to any state for use in violation of its laws, and the importation of alcoholic beverages in the mails is prohibited.

The United States adopted the metric system of measurement with the enactment of the Metric Conversion Act of 1975. In general, imported wine must conform with the metric standards of fill if bottled or packed on or after January 1, 1979. Imported distilled spirits, with some exceptions, must conform with the metric standards of fill if bottled or packed on or after January 1, 1980. Distilled spirits and wines bottled or packed prior to the respective dates must be accompanied by a statement to that effect signed by a duly authorized official of the appropriate foreign country. This statement may be a separate document or may be shown on the invoice. Malt beverages including beer are not subject to metric standards of fill.

MARKING

Imported wines in bottles and other containers are required to be packaged, marked, branded, and labeled in accordance with the regulations in 27 CFR Part 4. Imported malt beverages, including alcohol-free and nonalcoholic malt beverages, are also required to be labeled in conformance with the regulations in 27 CFR Part 7. The labeling regulations governing imported distilled spirits can be found in 27 CFR Part 5.

Each bottle, cask or other immediate container of imported distilled spirits, wines, or malt beverages must be marked for Customs purposes to indicate the country of origin of the alcoholic beverage contained therein, unless the shipment comes within one of the exceptions outlined in Chapter 29 of this book.

CERTIFICATE OF LABEL APPROVAL

Labels affixed to bottles of imported distilled spirits, wine and malt beverages must be covered by certificates of label approval issued to the importer by the Bureau of Alcohol, Tobacco and Firearms. Certificates of label approval or photostatic copies must be filed with Customs before the goods may be released for sale in the United States. Certificate-of-label approval requirements must also be met for fermented malt beverages if similar to the federal requirements (27 CFR Parts 4, 5 and 7).

FOREIGN DOCUMENTATION

Importers of wines and distilled spirits should consult the Bureau of Alcohol, Tobacco and Firearms about foreign documentation required, for example, certificates of origin,

age, etc. Wines or distilled spirits from certain countries require original certificates of origin as a condition of entry.

REQUIREMENTS OF OTHER AGENCIES

In addition, the importation of alcoholic beverages is subject to the specific requirements of the Food and Drug Administration. Certain plant materials, when used for bottle jackets for wine or other liquids, are subject to special restrictions under plant quarantine regulations of the Animal and Plant Health Inspection Service. All bottle jackets made of dried or unmanufactured plant materials are subject to inspection upon arrival and are referred to the Department of Agriculture.

Public Law 100-690, codified under 27 U.S.C. 213-219A, requires the following health warning to appear on the labels of containers of alcoholic beverages bottled on or after Nov. 18, 1989:

Government Warning: (1) According to the Surgeon General, women should not drink alcoholic beverages during pregnancy because of the risk of birth defects. (2) Consumption of alcoholic beverages impairs your ability to drive a car or operate machinery and may cause health problems.

35. MOTOR VEHICLES AND BOATS

AUTOMOBILES, VEHICLES AND VEHICLE EQUIPMENT

Safety, Bumper, and Emission Requirements. As a general rule, all imported motor vehicles less than 25 years old and items of motor vehicle equipment must comply with all applicable Federal Motor Vehicle Safety Standards in effect when these vehicles or items were manufactured. A Customs inspection at the time of entry will determine such compliance, which is verified by the original manufacturer's certification permanently affixed to the vehicle or merchandise. An entry declaration form, HS-7, must be filed when motor vehicles or items of motor

vehicle equipment are entered. The HS-7 can be obtained from customs brokers or ports of entry.

Certain temporary importations may be exempt from the requirements for conformance if written approval is obtained in advance from both the U.S. Department of Transportation and the Environmental Protection Agency. This includes vehicles brought in for research, demonstrations, investigation, studies, testing or competitive events. Also, EPA form 3520-1 and DOT form HS-7 must be submitted to Customs at the time entry is made for such vehicles.

Vehicles imported for temporary use by certain nonresidents or by members of foreign governments or foreign armed forces may not be required to comply with safety, bumper, emission, or theft-prevention standards. Nonconforming vehicles imported by nonresidents for personal use must be exported at the end of one year. Vehicles described in this paragraph may also require EPA and DOT declarations (forms 3520-1 and HS-7, respectively).

A DOT bond in the amount of 150 percent of the vehicle's dutiable value must be posted at the port of entry when a noncertified or nonconforming vehicle is imported for permanent use. The importer must also sign a contract with a DOT-registered importer, who will modify the vehicle to conform with all applicable safety and bumper standards, and who can certify the modification(s). A copy of this contract must be furnished to the Customs Service with the HS-7 at the port of entry. Furthermore, the vehicle model and model year must be determined to be eligible for importation.

For additional information or details on these requirements, contact the U.S. Department of Transportation, National Highway Traffic Safety Administration, Director of the Office of Vehicle Safety Compliance (NEF-32), 400 Seventh Street SW, Washington, DC 20590 Tel. (1-800) 424-9393.

The Clean Air Act, as amended, prohibits the importation of any motor vehicle or motor vehicle engine not in conformity with emission requirements prescribed by the U.S. Environmental Protection Agency (EPA). This restriction applies whether the motor vehicle or motor vehicle engine is new or used, and whether it was originally produced for sale and use in a foreign country or originally produced (or later modified) to conform to EPA requirements for sale or use in the United States. In addition to passenger cars, all trucks, multipurpose vehicles (e.g., all-terrain vehicles, campers), motorcycles, etc., that are capable of being registered by a state for use on public roads or that the EPA has deemed capable of being safely driven on public roads, are subject to these requirements. The term "vehicle" is used below to include all EPA-regulated vehicles and engines.

U.S.-Version Vehicles: Any person may import U.S.-version vehicles. *All such 1971 and later*

models are required to have a label in a readily visible position in the engine compartment stating that the vehicle conforms to U.S. requirements. This label will read "Vehicle Emission Control Information" and will have a statement by the manufacturer that the vehicle meets U.S. EPA emission requirements at the time of manufacture. If this label is not present, the importer should obtain a letter of conformity from the manufacturer's United States representative— not from a dealership—prior to importation.

Non-U.S.-Version Vehicles: Individuals are not permitted to import non-U.S.-version vehicles (unless otherwise excluded or exempted; see next sections). These vehicles must be imported (entered) by an Independent Commercial Importer (ICI) having a currently valid qualifying certificate of conformity for each vehicle being imported. The ICI will be responsible for performing all necessary modifications, testing and labeling, as well as providing an emissions warranty identical to the emissions warranty required of new vehicles sold in the U.S.

A list of approved ICIs is available from the EPA. Vehicles at least 21 years old are exempt from these provisions and may be imported without modification.

WORDS OF CAUTION:

- Not all nonconforming vehicles are eligible for importation, and ICIs are not required to accept vehicles for which they have qualifying certificates of conformity.

- EPA certification of ICIs does not guarantee the actions or work of the ICIs, nor does it regulate contractual agreements and working relationships with vehicle owners.

- EPA strongly recommends that prospective importers buy only U.S.-version (labeled) vehicles, because of the expense and potential difficulties involved with importing a non-U.S.-version vehicle.

- EPA strongly recommends that current owners of non-U.S.-version vehicles sell or otherwise dispose of them overseas rather than ship and import them into the U.S., because of the expense and potential difficulties involved with importing a non-U.S.-version vehicle.

- Before shipping a nonconforming vehicle for importation, EPA strongly recommends that the importer either make final arrangements with an ICI for modifications and testing or obtain EPA approval in writing for importation. Storage fees at the ports are costly, and the vehicle may not be eligible for importation.

- The EPA policy that permitted importers a one-time exemption for vehicles at least five years old has been eliminated.

- EPA considers a U.S.-version vehicle that has had modifications to its drive train or emission control system to be a non-U.S.-version vehicle, even though it may be labeled a U.S.-version vehicle.

For Further Information: Environmental Protection Agency, Investigation/Imports Section (6405-J), Washington, DC 20460; Tel. (202) 564-9660; Fax (202) 565-2057.

Final Word of Caution. *Modifications necessary to bring a nonconforming vehicle into conformity with the safety, bumper, or emission standards may require extensive engineering, be impractical or impossible, or the labor and materials may be unduly expensive. It is highly recommended that these modifications be investigated before a vehicle is purchased for importation.*

BOAT SAFETY STANDARDS

Imported boats and associated equipment are subject to U.S. Coast Guard safety regulations or standards under the Federal Boat Safety Act of 1971. Products subject to standards must have a compliance certification label affixed to them. Certain hulls also require a hull identification number to be affixed. A U.S. Coast Guard import declaration is required to be filed with entries of nonconforming boats. Further information may be obtained from the Commandant, U.S. Coast Guard, Washington, DC 20593.

DUTIABILITY

Vessels brought into the United States for use in trade or commerce are not dutiable. Yachts or pleasure boats brought into the United States by nonresidents for their own use in pleasure cruising are also not dutiable. Yachts or pleasure boats owned by a resident or brought into the United States for sale or charter to a resident are dutiable. Further information may be found in the U.S. Customs pamphlet *Pleasure Boats*.

RESTRICTIONS ON USE

Vessels that are foreign-built or of foreign registry may be used in the United States for pleasure purposes and in the foreign trade of the United States. However, Federal law prohibits the use of such vessels in the coastwise trade, i.e., the transportation of passengers or merchandise between points in the United States, including carrying fishing parties for hire. Questions concerning the use of foreign-built or foreign-flag vessels should be addressed to:

Chief, Entry and Carrier Rulings Branch
Office of Regulations and Rulings
U.S. Customs Service
1300 Pennsylvania Avenue NW
Washington, DC 20229

36. IMPORT QUOTAS

An import quota is a quantity control on imported merchandise for a certain period of time. Quotas are established by legislation, by directives, and by proclamations issued under the authority contained in specific legislation. The majority of import quotas are administered by the U.S. Customs Service. The Commissioner of Customs controls the importation of quota merchandise but has no authority to change or modify any quota.

United States import quotas may be divided into two types: *absolute* and *tariff-rate*. Under the North American Free Trade Agreement (NAFTA), there are tariff-preference levels, which are administered like tariff-rate quotas.

Tariff-rate quotas provide for the entry of a specified quantity of the quota product at a reduced rate of duty during a given period. There is no limitation on the amount of the product that may be entered during the quota period, but quantities entered in excess of the quota for the period are subject to higher duty rates. In most cases, products of Communist-controlled areas are not entitled to the benefits of tariff-rate quotas.

Absolute quotas are quantitative, that is, no more than the amount specified may be permitted entry during a quota period. Some absolute quotas are global, while others are allocated to specified foreign countries. Imports in excess of a specified quota may be held for the opening of the next quota period by placing it in a foreign trade zone or by entering it for warehouse, or it may be exported or destroyed under Customs supervision.

The usual Customs procedures generally applicable to other imports apply with respect to commodities subject to quota limitations.

The quota status of a commodity subject to a tariff-rate quota cannot be determined in advance of its entry. The quota rates of duty are ordinarily assessed on such commodities entered from the beginning of the quota period until such time in the period as it is determined that imports are nearing the quota level. Port directors of Customs are then instructed to require the deposit of estimated duties at the over-quota duty rate and to report the time of official presentation of each entry. A final determination is then made of the date and time when a quota is filled, and all port directors are advised accordingly.

Some of the absolute quotas are invariably filled at or shortly after the opening of the quota period. Each of these quotas is therefore officially opened at 12 noon Eastern Standard Time, or the equivalent in other time zones, on the designated effective date. When the total quantity for these entries filed at the opening of the quota period exceeds the quota, the merchandise is released on a pro rata basis, the pro rata being the ratio between the quota quantity and the total quantity offered for entry. This assures an equitable distribution of the quota.

Merchandise is not regarded as presented for purposes of determining quota priority until an entry summary or withdrawal from warehouse for consumption has been submitted in proper form and the merchandise is located within the port limits.

COMMODITIES SUBJECT TO QUOTAS ADMINISTERED BY CUSTOMS

As provided in the Harmonized Tariff Schedule of the United States, the commodities listed below are subject to quota limitations in effect as of the date of publication of this book. Local Customs officers can be consulted about any changes.

Information may also be obtained by contacting the Quota Staff, U.S. Customs Service, 1300 Pennsylvania Avenue NW, Washington, DC 20229, (202) 927–5850.

Tariff-Rate Quotas

- 0401.20.20—Milk and cream
- 1604.16—Anchovies
- 9603—Brooms
- 9903.96—Broom corn brooms
- 9901.00.50—Ethyl alcohol

- Chapter 20—Olives
- 2008.30.42—Satsumas (mandarins)
- 1604.14.20—Tuna
- 9903.52—Upland cotton
- Chapter 24, AUSN 5—Tobacco
- 9903.11—Wheat gluten (Absolute)

NAFTA

Presidential Proclamation 6641 implemented the North American Free Trade Agreement and established tariff-preference levels on the following qualifying imported goods:

Imported from Mexico:

- Chapter 99, Subchapter VI, U.S. Note 4 (99 USN 4)—Milk and cream
- 99 USN 5—Dried milk and dried cream
- 99 USN 6—Dried milk and dried cream
- 99 USN 7—Milk and cream (condensed and evaporated)
- 99 USN 8—Cheese
- 99 USN 9—Tomatoes
- 99 USN 10—Tomatoes
- 99 USN 11—Onions and shallots
- 99 USN 12—Eggplants
- 99 USN 13—Chili peppers
- 99 USN 14—Squash
- 99 USN 15—Watermelons
- 99 USN 16—Peanuts
- 99 USN 18—Sugars derived from sugar cane or sugar beets
- 99 USN 19—Blended syrups
- 99 USN 20—Sugars derived from sugar cane or sugar beets
- 99 USN 21—Orange juice
- 99 USN 22—Orange juice
- 99 USN 25—Cotton
- 9906.96.01—Brooms
- Section XI Additional U.S. Notes—cotton or man-made fiber apparel, wool apparel, cotton or man-made fiber fabrics and made-ups and cotton or man-made fibers yarns.

Imported from Canada:

- Section XI Additional U.S. Notes—cotton or man-made fiber apparel, wool apparel, cotton or man-made fiber fabrics and made-ups and cotton or man-made fibers yarns.

Tariff-Rate Quotas—GATT:

Presidential Proclamation 6763 implemented the GATT Uruguay Round Agreements for the following tariff-rate commodities:

- Chapter 2, Additional U.S. Note 3 (2 AUSN 3)—Beef
- 4 AUSN 5—Milk and cream
- 4 AUSN 9—Dried milk and dried cream
- 4 AUSN 10—Dairy products
- 4 AUSN 11—Milk and cream (condensed or evaporated)
- 4 AUSN 12—Dried milk, dried cream, and dried whey (in excess of 224,981 kilograms)
- 4 AUSN 18—Canadian cheddar cheese
- 12 AUSN 2—Peanuts
- 17 AUSN 5—Sugar (including sugar cane)
- 17 AUSN 7—Articles containing more than 65 percent by dry weight of sugar described in 17 AUSN 2
- 17 AUSN 8—Articles containing more than 10 percent by dry weight of sugar described in 17 AUSN 3
- 17 AUSN 9—Blended syrups
- 18 AUSN 1—Cocoa powder
- 18 AUSN 2—Chocolate
- 18 AUSN 3—Chocolate and low-fat chocolate crumb
- 19 AUSN 2—Infant formula
- 19 AUSN 3—Mixes and doughs
- 20 AUSN 5—Peanut butter and paste
- 21 AUSN 4—Mixed condiments and mixed seasonings
- 21 AUSN 5—Ice cream
- 23 AUSN 2—Animal feed
- 52 AUSN 5—Cotton
- 52 AUSN 6—Harsh or rough cotton

- 52 AUSN 7—Cotton
- 52 AUSN 8—Cotton
- 52 AUSN 9—Card strips made from cotton
- 52 AUSN 10—Fibers of cotton

Tariff-Rate Quotas: U.S.-Israel Agreement on Trade in Agricultural Products

Presidential Proclamation 6962 implemented the U.S.-Israel agreement for the following agricultural products:

- Chapter 99, Subchapter VIII, U.S. Note 3—Butter, fresh or sour cream
- Chapter 99, Subchapter VIII, U.S. Note 4—Dried milk
- Chapter 99, Subchapter VIII, U.S. Note 5—Cheese and substitutes for cheese
- Chapter 99, Subchapter VIII, U.S. Note 6—Peanuts
- Chapter 99, Subchapter VIII, U.S. Note 7—Ice cream

TEXTILE ARTICLES

The U.S. Customs Service administers import controls on certain cotton, wool, man-made fiber, silk blend and other vegetable-fiber articles manufactured or produced in designated countries. The U.S. Customs Service administers the Special Access Program and the Andean Trade Preference Act on certain products which are made of U.S.-formed-and-cut fabric. These controls are imposed on the basis of directives issued to the Commissioner of Customs by the Chairman of the Committee for the Implementation of Textile Agreements.

Information concerning specific import controls may be obtained from the Commissioner of Customs. Other information concerning the textile program may be obtained from the Chairman, Committee for the Implementation of Textile Agreements, U.S. Department of Commerce, Washington, DC 20230.

Textile Visa and Export License Requirements

A textile visa is an endorsement in the form of a stamp on an invoice or export control license that is executed by a foreign government. It is used to control the exportation of textiles and textile products to the United States and to prohibit the unauthorized entry of the merchandise into this country. A visa may cover either quota or nonquota merchandise. Conversely, quota merchandise may or may not require a visa depending upon the country of origin. A visa does not guarantee entry of the merchandise into the United States. If the quota closes between the time the visa is issued in the foreign country and the shipment's arrival in the United States, the shipment will not be released to the importer until the quota opens again.

Electronic Visa Information System (ELVIS)

ELVIS is the electronic transmission of visa information for textile merchandise from a specific country to the U.S. Customs Service.

QUOTAS OR LICENSES ADMINISTERED BY OTHER GOVERNMENT AGENCIES

Watches and Watch Movements. There are no licensing requirements or quotas on watches and watch movements entering the United States unless the watches and watch movements are produced in the insular possessions (U.S. Virgin Islands, American Samoa, Guam). The Departments of Commerce and the Interior administer a program that establishes an annual allocation for watches and watch movements assembled in the insular possessions to enter the United States free of duty under statistical notes (91/5) to Chapter 91 of the Harmonized Tariff Schedule. Licenses are issued only to established insular producers. Further information on the insular watch program may be obtained from the Statutory Import Programs Staff, Import Administration, U.S. Department of Commerce, Washington, DC 20230.

Dairy Products. Certain dairy products are subject to annual import quotas administered by the Department of Agriculture and may be imported at the in-quota rate only under import licenses issued by that department. Detailed information on the licensing of these products, or the conditions under which limited quantities of the products may be imported without licenses, may be obtained from the Dairy

Import Group, Foreign Agricultural Service, U.S. Department of Agriculture, Washington, DC 20250, (202) 720–9439.

- Chapter 4, Additional U.S. Note 6 (4 AUSN 6)—Butter and fresh or sour cream
- 4 AUSN 7—Dried milk
- 4 AUSN 8—Dried milk or dried cream
- 4 AUSN 12—Dried milk, dried cream or dried whey (up to 224,981 kilograms)
- 4 AUSN 14—Butter substitutes
- 4 AUSN 16—Cheeses and substitutes for cheese
- 4 AUSN 17—Blue-molded cheese
- 4 AUSN 18—Cheddar cheese (except Canadian cheddar)
- 4 AUSN 19—American-type cheese
- 4 AUSN 20—Edam and Gouda cheese
- 4 AUSN 21—Italian-type cheese
- 4 AUSN 22—Swiss or Emmentaler cheese
- 4 AUSN 23—Cheese and substitutes for cheese
- 4 AUSN 25—Swiss or Emmentaler cheese

The above products may be imported at the over-quota rate without an import license.

37. CIVIL AND CRIMINAL ENFORCEMENT PROVISIONS

Section 592 of the Tariff Act of 1930, as amended (19 U.S.C. 1592), generally provides that any person who by fraud, gross negligence, or negligence, enters, introduces, or attempts to introduce merchandise into the commerce of the United States by means of any material and false electronically transmitted data, written or oral statement, document or act, or by any omission which is material, will be subject to a monetary penalty. In limited circumstances, the person's merchandise may be seized to insure payment of the penalty, and forfeited if the penalty is not paid.

The civil fraud statute has been applied by the Customs Service in cases involving individuals and companies in the United States and abroad that have negligently or intentionally provided false information concerning importations into the United States.

A criminal fraud statute also provides for sanctions to those presenting false information to Customs officers. Title 18, United States Code, Section 542, provides a maximum of two years' imprisonment, a fine, or both, for each violation involving an importation or attempted importation. Both the civil and criminal fraud statutes were enacted by Congress to discourage persons from evading the payment of lawful duties owed to the United States, although these laws apply today whether or not the United States is deprived of lawful duties.

In addition, under Section 596 of the Tariff Act of 1930, as amended (19 U.S.C. 1595a(c), the Customs Service is required to seize and forfeit all merchandise which is stolen or smuggled, as well as controlled substances and certain contraband articles. Merchandise may be seized and forfeited if: its importation is restricted or prohibited because of a law relating to health,

safety or conservation; the merchandise is lacking a federal license required for the importation; the merchandise or packaging is in violation of copyright, trademark, trade name, or trade dress protections; the merchandise is intentionally or repetitively marked in violation of country of origin marking requirements; or the importation of the merchandise is subject to quantitative restrictions requiring a visa or similar document from a foreign government, and the document presented with the entry is counterfeit.

Additionally, federal laws relating to criminal activities commonly known as "money laundering" created criminal and civil provisions that, along with fines and imprisonment, enable the government to prosecute persons for, and to seize and forfeit property involved in or traceable to, violations of the Money Laundering Control Act or Bank Secrecy Act. Importation fraud violations are included as specified unlawful activities or predicate offenses within the Money Laundering Control Act. Criminal penalties include imprisonment for up to 20 years for each offense and fines of up to $500,000, or both, and/or a civil penalty up to twice the value of the property involved in the offense.

The criminal and civil fraud statutes, as well as money laundering statutes, are all enforced by special agents assigned to the Office of Investigations; they operate throughout the United States and in the world's major trading centers. Suspected or known violations of any law involved with the importation of merchandise into the United States can be reported toll-free and anonymously by calling 1-800-BE-ALERT (1-800-232-5378). Rewards are applicable in many instances associated with the reporting of fraud.

38. FOREIGN TRADE ZONES

Foreign or "free" trade zones are secured areas legally outside a nation's customs territory. Their purpose is to attract and promote international trade and commerce. The Foreign Trade Zones Board authorizes operations within these zones based upon showing that the intended operations are not detrimental to the public interest. Subzones are special-purpose facilities for companies unable to operate effectively at public zone sites. Foreign trade zones are usually located in or near Customs ports of entry, at industrial parks or terminal warehouse facilities. Foreign trade zones must be within 60 miles or 90 minutes' driving time from the port of entry limits, while subzones have no limit and are located in the zone user's private facility. A Foreign Trade Zones Board, created by the Foreign Trade Zones Act of 1934, reviews and approves applications to establish, operate, and maintain foreign trade zones. It is important to note that although foreign trade zones are treated as being outside the customs territory of the United States for tariff and customs entry purposes, all other federal laws, such as the Federal Food, Drug, and Cosmetic Act, are applicable to products and establishments within such zones.

Foreign exporters planning to expand or open up new American outlets may forward their goods to a foreign trade zone in the United States to be held for an unlimited period while awaiting a favorable market in the United States or nearby countries without being subject to customs entry, payment of duty or tax, or bond.

TREATMENT OF GOODS

Merchandise lawfully brought into these zones may be stored, sold, exhibited, broken up, repacked, assembled, distributed, sorted, graded, cleaned, mixed with foreign or domestic merchandise, or otherwise manipulated or manufactured. However, merchandise imported for use

in the zone, such as construction material and production equipment, must be entered for consumption before it is taken into a zone. The Foreign Trade Zones Board may determine, however, that an operation is not in the public interest. The resulting merchandise may thereafter be either exported or transferred into the customs territory. When foreign goods, in their condition at time of entry into the zone or after processing there, are transferred into the customs territory of the United States, the goods must be entered at the customs house. If entered for consumption, duties and taxes will be assessed on the entered articles according to the condition of the foreign merchandise at the time of entry from the zone, if the merchandise has been placed in nonprivileged foreign status prior to manipulation or manufacture.

The owner of foreign merchandise that has not been manipulated or manufactured in any way that would effect a change in its U.S. tariff classification had it been taken into customs territory when first imported, may, upon request to the port director of Customs, have its dutiable status fixed and liquidated. This dutiable status will apply regardless of when the merchandise is entered into customs territory and even though its condition or form may have been changed by processing in the zone, as indicated above. Merchandise may be considered exported, for customs or other purposes, upon its admission to a zone in zone-restricted status; however, the merchandise taken into a zone under zone-restricted status may be for the sole purpose of exportation, destruction (except destruction of distilled spirits, wines, and fermented malt liquors) or storage.

An important feature of foreign trade zones for foreign merchants entering the American market is that the goods may be brought to the threshold of the market, making immediate delivery certain and avoiding possible cancellation of orders due to shipping delays after a favorable market has closed.

Production of articles in zones by the combined use of domestic and foreign materials makes it unnecessary to send the domestic materials abroad for manufacture, or to pay duty or obtain a bond for foreign materials that have been imported for this purpose. Duties on the foreign goods involved in such processing or manufacture are payable only on the actual quantity of such foreign goods incorporated into merchandise transferred from a zone for entry into the commerce of the United States. If there is any unrecoverable waste resulting from manufacture or manipulation, allowances are made for it, thereby eliminating payment of duty except on the articles that are actually entered. If there is any recoverable waste, it is dutiable only in its condition as such and in the quantity entered.

The Foreign Trade Zones Act also authorizes the exhibiting of merchandise within a zone. Zone facilities may be utilized for the full exhibition of foreign merchandise without bond, for an unlimited length of time, and with no requirement of exportation or duty payment. Thus, the owner of goods in a zone may display the goods where they are stored, establish showrooms of her own, or join with other importers in displaying his merchandise in a permanent exhibition established in the zone, and since the importer may also store and process merchandise in a zone, he is not limited to mere display of samples, but may sell from stock in wholesale quantities. Retail trade is prohibited in zones.

Domestic merchandise may be taken into a zone and, providing its identity is maintained in accordance with regulations, may be returned to customs territory free of quotas, duty, or tax, even though while in the zone it may have been combined with or made part of other articles. However, domestic distilled spirits, wine, and beer, and a limited number of other kinds of merchandise generally may not be processed while in the zone.

ADVANTAGES

Savings may result from manipulations and manufacture in a zone. For example, many

products shipped to the zone in bulk can be dried, sorted, graded, or cleaned and bagged or packed, permitting savings of duties and taxes on moisture taken from content or on dirt removed and culls thrown out. From incoming shipments of packaged or bottled goods, damaged packages or broken bottles can be removed. Where evaporation results during shipment or while goods are stored in the zone, contents of barrels or other containers can be regauged and savings obtained, as no duties are payable on the portions lost or removed. In other words, barrels or other containers can be gauged at the time of transfer to customs territory to insure that duties will not be charged on any portion of their contents lost to evaporation, leakage, breakage, or otherwise. These operations may also be conducted in bonded warehouses.

Savings in shipping charges, duties, and taxes may result from such operations as shipping unassembled or disassembled furniture, machinery, etc., to the zone and assembling or reassembling it there.

Merchandise may be remarked or relabeled in the zone (or in a bonded warehouse) to conform to requirements for entry into the commerce of the United States if it is otherwise up to standard. Remarking or relabeling that would be misleading is not permitted in the zone. Substandard foods and drugs may, in certain cases, be reconditioned to meet the requirements of the Food, Drug, and Cosmetics Act.

There is no time limit as to how long foreign merchandise may be stored in a zone, or when it must be entered into customs territory, reexported, or destroyed.

TRANSFER OF GOODS IN BONDED WAREHOUSES

Foreign merchandise in Customs bonded warehouses may be transferred to the zone at any time before its retention date in the bonded warehouse expires, but such a transfer may be made only for the purpose of eventual exportation, destruction, or permanent storage.

When foreign merchandise is transferred to the zone from Customs bonded warehouses, the bond is cancelled and all obligations regarding duty payment, or the time when merchandise must be reexported, are terminated. Similarly, the owner of domestic merchandise stored in Internal Revenue bonded warehouses may transfer his or her goods to a zone and obtain cancellation of bonds. In addition, domestic goods moved into a zone under zone-restricted status are, upon entering the zone, considered exported for purposes of excise and other internal revenue tax rebates. A manufacturer operating in customs territory and using dutiable imported materials in his or her product may, upon transferring the product to the zone for export and complying with appropriate regulations, also obtain drawback of duties paid or cancellation of bond.

Location of and general information on United States foreign trade zones may be obtained from the Foreign Trade Zones Board, Department of Commerce, Washington, DC 20330. Questions relating to legal aspects of Customs Service responsibilities in regard to foreign trade zones should be addressed to: Chief, Entry and Carrier Rulings Branch, U.S. Customs Service, Washington, DC 20229. Questions relating to the operational aspects of such responsibilities should be addressed to the appropriate port director of Customs. The Foreign Trade Zones Manual for grantees, operators, users, or customs brokers may be purchased from Superintendent of Documents, U.S. Government Printing Office, Washington, DC 20402. When ordering refer to GPO Stock No. 048-002-00128-1 and Customs Publication No. 559.

The Foreign Trade Zones Manual may also be viewed at, or downloaded from, the Customs Service's Web site at **www.customs.ustreas.gov**.

Tax Havens for the International Trader

byAdam Starchild

Tax havens are very much in the news, and stories about small- and medium-sized companies mushrooming overnight and multi-national giants amassing fabulous fortunes via tax haven operations are growing. They may sound like Alice in Wonderland fairy tales to most people, but to the sophisticated entrepreneur, use of foreign tax havens for such advantages is an

everyday business opportunity.

The use of a foreign corporation domiciled in any one of the famous company tax havens such as Switzerland, Panama, Hong Kong, or Bermuda (among others, can enhance the profitability of any international business, and especially a travel or tourism enterprise.

Many European and American companies are expanding and diversifying overseas as a means of growth and as a hedge against economic ups and downs in their country of origin. By incorporating a tax haven operation to accumulate tax-free income, accomplishment of multi-national objectives is accelerated. An international trading or freight operation can be established in a tax haven to be used as a conduit for international sales activity and financing. Such operations can accumulate trade discounts, commissions, advertising allowances, etc., completely tax-free while the parent or associated company can assume tax deductions by absorbing administrative and selling costs.

Before getting into the ways in which tax haven operations are used by various types of businesses, it is of eminent importance that the distinct difference is understood between two seemingly similar terms: "tax avoidance" and "tax evasion." Tax evasion has dubious and illegal overtones: for example, a company might falsify its financial statements so as to conceal its full liability to the tax authorities — that would be tax evasion — an infraction of the law and a very serious one.

Tax avoidance, on the other hand, is a legitimate method of minimizing or negating the tax factor. In simple terms, it is utilizing "loopholes" in tax laws and exploiting them within legal perimeters. This is the cornerstone of the tax haven concept.

Certain offshore companies can defer any tax until the profits are repatriated to the investor's home country. These are generally companies actively engaged in the conduct of a local business. In most import-export or other international trade activities, such a definition is especially easy to meet. A retailer, or group of retailers, could set up their own wholesale buying opertion in a convenient tax haven, such as Hong Kong, and put all of their Asian business through it. The profits of the Hong Kong firm would accumulate tax-free, and could be invested in other foreign operations.

In addition, a great many countries offer tax holidays of 5 to 20 years for new export manufacturers or assembly operations, often including smaller companies down to as few as ten employees. A company or group of companies could easily invest some of their foreign profits in such a venture, continuing to build for tax-free profits. Such concessions often include an exemption from customs duties on raw materials and equipment.

Most developed countries do tax the current income of certain types of corporations controlled by their residents, such as leasing companies, and other financial enterprises dealing the parent company. But this concept of a controlled foreign corporation applies usually to passive or tax-haven type corporations, not to active businesses. But even for a passive business, a joint venture with foreign partners on a 50-50 basis will allow the income to accumulate tax-free since the company is not controlled by national of either country. If you are leasing equipment, consider a joint venture with your foreign partner whereby you set up a jointly owned company to receive some of the income. You will both profit by it, and have a tax-free pool of funds to invest together in other ventures. Such profits will not be taxed in the country of either partner until they are repatriated, since they are not controlled by either country's citizen.

Countries which have no income tax include Bermuda, the Bahamas, the Cayman Islands, Nevis, and the Turks & Caicos Islands. A number of countries do not tax foreign source income, including Panama and Hong Kong. Shannon International Airport in Ireland also has special concessions for service companies setting up in the airport area.

Many businessmen looking for tax haven opportunities would envy the daily opportunities open to international traders, and yet most international traders rarely use these opportunities — or even understand them. 100% tax-free dollars will grow a whole lot faster than 50% after-tax dollars.

Setting Up Your Tax Haven-Based Trading Operation

There are two companies that I can personally highly recommend for assistance in exploiting the extensive possibilities in using tax havens for international business.

The first is Skye Fiduciary Services Limited, based in the Isle of Man, are specialist consultants, designers and trustees and managers of offshore and international fiduciary structures.

They were established in 1991 by Charles Cain to provide specialist consultancy and management services in respect of offshore fiduciary structures, specializing in clients from or connected to the USA. The beginnings of Skye Fiduciary Services Limited go back over twenty

years. In 1972, their Executive Chairman, Charles Cain, after some years working in international banking in East Africa and the United Kingdom, returned to his native country as the managing director of a merchant bank. Three years later he resigned to start his own business, which became, by 1989, the largest corporate and trust management business in the Isle of Man. In 1989, however, as a consequence of an illness, he sold out to a large financial services group.

In 1991, fully recovered, he established Skye Fiduciary Services Limited.

From its executive office in the Isle of Man, Skye Fiduciary Services Limited provides a design and management service relating to offshore companies and trusts.

Unlike many firms that simply provide offshore corporations, one of Sky's major functions is to provide trade management services. These include:
• arranging and supervising appropriate banking and trade finance facilities and services.
  • trade documentation
  • exchange control planning
  • double tax treaty planning.
  • administration of trading entities
  • arranging bank Letters of Credit and other financial instruments
  • arranging leasing, invoice discounting and credit factoring

- arranging tax efficient vehicles for transferring royalties and other income flows derived from intellectual property rights.
  - offshore joint venture vehicles and holding structures for US persons
  - international trading structures.

> For more information contact:
> Skye Fiduciary Services Limited
> Attn: New Clients Information
> 2 Water Street
> Ramsey, Isle of Man 1M8 1JP
> Great Britain
> Telephone: +44 1624 816117
> Fax: +44 1624 816645; attn: New Clients Information

The other firm I can personally give my highest recommendation to is ICS Trust (Asia) Limited, based in Hong Kong.

The handover of the former British Crown Colony of Hong Kong to China is complete, and it is now called the Hong Kong Special Administrative Region, generally abbreviated to Hong Kong S.A.R., even on official documents.

As more than one local businessman has put it, "now that the politicians and journalists are gone (from covering the handover), we can get down to *business.*" This attitude is typical of Hong Kong, still a true capitalist center. In fact, many of the wealthy who left to obtain second citizenships in Canada, Australia, and elsewhere, have now returned home to continue building their fortunes.

Offshore re invoicing can be a very useful tool for exporters as well as importers, since it allows for the accumulation of tax free profits in an offshore environment.

Through re invoicing, an offshore corporation is established as an international intermediary between importers and their suppliers or between exporters and their customers. The offshore corporation can thus either 1) buy products, on behalf of the importer, at the

negotiated price level and then sell, or re invoice, these same products to the importer at a higher price, thereby accumulating profits offshore where there is no tax liability and significantly

reducing profits in the country of destination where there is tax liability, or 2) buy products at discount prices from the exporter, thereby creating a very small profit in the exporting country with tax liability and sell, or re invoice, these same products at market value prices to overseas buyers, thereby accumulating profits offshore where there is no tax liability.

In order to be profitable, offshore re invoicing operations need to be situated in an environment where import export transactions are either tax free or low tax (in relation to the onshore portion of the operation).

Once the offshore company has been established, the management corporation needs to acquire the services of a post office box, a telex, a telephone, and a facsimile for its use. When all this is in place, the management company can begin re invoicing. An offshore service provider can arrange these services.

The merchandise can be sent directly to the exporter's client or to the importer. The only functions performed in the offshore haven are the preparation and dispatch of the new invoice and the management of the funds in the way instructed by the client and complying with local regulations.

The major advantage of Hong Kong is simply that it is a real business center, not just a tax haven. One of the consequences of that is the ability to add value to services that are provided in only skeleton form in other tax havens. The reinvoicing business is a prime example. Most tax haven jurisdictions host a number of trading companies that do nothing more than reinvoicing. But one Hong Kong firm has now developed this traditional service into a "real" business mode, with an ability to arrange local trade financing. This is a healthy step away from traditional tax havenry into a true offshore business center.

ICS Trust Company Limited is part of the ICS International group of companies headquartered in Hong Kong. This highly successful entrepreneurial group was started by Elizabeth L. Thomson. Elizabeth describes herself as "a lawyer by profession" (2 law degrees, a member of 4 Law Societies internationally), "an entrepreneur by choice"! She has helped innumerable people start new enterprises in many parts of the globe and is well known in Hong Kong for her work with women entrepreneurs.

With a staff of 40 at ICS, every aspect of your business is covered — from deciding to incorporate, to obtaining financing from the bank, to managing your paper work including Letters of Credit, to investing your hard earned profits! ICS is truly a "one stop shop" for entrepreneurs.

Their clients range from multinational companies for whom they run Direct Import Programs worth millions of dollars to individuals who seek tax sheltering and estate planning on an international scale. As an entrepreneurial group, they attract many entrepreneurs as clients — business people who have grown their business to a level of maturity and profits that requires expansion into Asia for many diverse reasons.

Instead of just a paper thin traditional tax haven reinvoicing company, with ICS you can develop a real business in Hong Kong. With their extensive banking contacts, ICS professionals will "shop" for the best letter of credit facilities that Hong Kong's competitive banking scene can offer, likely better facilities than you can find at home. Depending upon the client, ICS can often arrange letter of credit banking facilities for clients with either a low or zero margin deposit, usually required by the opening bank. By freeing up your collateral and capital, they provide you with more purchasing power to increase sales and gain higher profits.

Most of these reinvoicing transactions are usually effected such that they are tax free in Hong Kong. There is no withholding tax on dividends so it is often possible to engage in international trade through a HK company and obtain dividends from that company tax free.

ICS will also work with international banks and factors in Hong Kong and overseas to arrange financing, secured primarily on the strength of purchase orders from your clients. Working with banks, factories, shipping companies and freight forwarders, ICS will structure a transaction to increase the likelihood of obtaining flexible, low cost facilities.

The goods do not need to go through HK for us to use a HK vehicle to pass title. Most of their clients ship from a third country direct to their own country.

Although the traditional Hong Kong focus is on firms who trade in goods, it is also possible to use these structures in cases where services are to be provided from overseas. For example, a firm could contract out a study to a company in Hong Kong. This Hong Kong company could then sub contract out the work to a third party firm and the profit kept in Hong Kong, tax free.

If you import goods from Asia for sale to large chains, ICS can help you expand your credit facilities and increase your domestic sales by establishing and running a Direct Import Program for you. Combined with their international trade finance capabilities, the Direct Import Program is a powerful tool for generating more profits.

The primary goal of the Direct Import Program is to maximize your profits by making your customers perceive that they are buying "direct." This is achieved by:

- setting up a subsidiary company in Hong Kong
- getting your buyers to open their L/C or orders to this subsidiary
- liaising with suppliers to ensure goods are to specification.

The Direct Import Program works because of two powerful reasons:

- The trend in the retail industry is for buyers to "buy direct" from the Orient. Having a subsidiary in Hong Kong which receives orders or L/Cs greatly enhances this perception.
- Large retail chains often can obtain freight and insurance at significant savings because of their economies of scale. Selling FOB Asia can often result in a lower selling price for the importer but with the same profit.

ICS will set up and manage the subsidiary company for you, and prepare financing proposals for presentation to local banks. When everything is complete, goods are shipped directly from the Asian factory to the customer. The fact that you are now seen as an Asian supplier (and not the middleman) is often an important factor that clinches the deal. The added prestige of a Hong Kong office makes the customer think he or she is buying "direct" and therefore receiving the lowest price.

To get started, you should contact ICS with as much detail as possible about your business and its trading activities.

For further information, contact:
Mr. Kishore K. Sakhrani
Director
ICS Trust (Asia) Limited
8th Floor, Henley Building
Five Queens's Road, Central
Hong Kong
Telephone: +852 2854 4544
Fax: +852 2543 5555

You will be well-advised and well-serviced in the hands of either of these fine companies.

About the Author

Over the past 25 years, Adam Starchild has been the author of over two dozen books, and hundreds of magazine articles, primarily on business and finance. His articles have appeared in a wide range of publications around the world † including Business Credit, Euromoney, Finance, The Financial Planner, International Living, Offshore Financial Review, Reason, Tax Planning International, The Bull & Bear, Trust & Estates, and many more.

Now semi retired, he was the president of an international consulting group specializing in banking, finance and the development of new businesses, and director of a trust company.

Although this formidable testimony to expertise in his field, plus his current preoccupation with other books in progress, would not seem to leave time for a well rounded existence, Starchild has won two Presidential Sports Awards and written several cookbooks, and is currently involved in a number of personal charitable projects.

His personal website is at http://www.adamstarchild.com/

Exporting -- The Fastest Way to Grow a Small Manufacturing Business!

by J. F. (Jim) Straw

When most small manufacturing businesses start-up, they concentrate their sales efforts on the known markets here in the U.S. Defining their markets as the known users of their products; known distributors of those products; and known, or accessible, sales areas within the U.S., overlooking the larger, more profitable, markets outside this country.

Most small manufacturers who do investigate the possibilities of exporting their products **give up** after reading a number of Department of Commerce publications detailing the intricacies of export documentation, freight forwarding, and international banking instruments. (The same complex, intricate processing, paperwork jungle, methods I studied when I was 18 years old... and discareded after I made my first real sale overseas.)

What the Department of Commerce... and other learned sources... fail to tell you is that **all** of the necessary documentation, freight forwarding, and international banking aspects of exporting can be handled — easily and cheaply — by professional service providers who do it every day. As a matter of fact, the "cost" of those services is so negligible it usually isn't even necessary to make a provision for them in your pricing structure.

Exporting is, really, no more difficult than marketing your products here in the U.S. All you have to do is... **Make a Sale**... **Get Paid**... and **Ship Your Product**. The rest of the procedures can be handled, inexpensively, by the customary service providers.

Beyond that, exporting can allow a small manufacturing company to grow... almost exponentially... because you will experience:

Larger Orders — Importers in other countries won't just buy one or two of your products (unless they are ordering samples). Due to the added costs of freight, insurance, and customs duties in their countries, they will order in bigger and bigger volume in order to reduce the per piece cost.

Easier Financing — Since export orders are (almost always) accompanied by some method of payment... Letter of Credit, Sight or Bank Draft, etc... your local banker will (usually) be willing to advance funds against that documentation. Beyond that, both State and Federal Governments offer a wide variety of financing incentives... everything from free grants to production financing... for exporters. And, even the smallest of companies can qualify for that financing because the financial strength of the foreign buyer, not the manufacturing company, determines the creditability of the transaction.

Limited Competition — No matter what you manufacture, you won't have the heavy competition you might face here in the U.S. Statistically, less than 20% of the manufacturers in this country export their products — and — of those companies that do export, fully 50% of them *only* export to one (1) foreign country. So, even if one of your competitors is exporting, the odds are you can still be the ONLY supplier in a number of other countries... without competition.

The only concern then is...

HOW TO MAKE THE SALES

...but, just as there are Manufacturer's Representatives in the U.S. who will take a manufacturer's products directly to the distributors, there are international Manufacturer's Reps who will do the same thing for your company in the marketplace of the world.

Usually, the employment of an International Manufacturer's Rep doesn't take any "out of pocket" money... other than the provision of your usual printed materials, catalog sheets and brochures. Like Manufacturer's Reps in the U.S., International Manufacturer's Reps pay their own way and earn commissions based solely upon the sale of your products. But, unlike their domestic counterparts, Internnational Manufacturer's Reps cn, and do, assist the manufacturers in accessing necessary service providers, freight forwarders, banking and financing.

Exporting truly is the fastest... and easiest... way to grow a small manufacturing business. Just one export order can turn a small manufacturer into a mid-size manufacturer, virtually overnight. As an exporter and international manufacturer's rep for well over 30 years... with clients and customers in over 70 countries... I've seen it happen countless times. So...

If you are a manufacturer... looking to expand your business, exponentially... investigate Exporting today. — It's much easier than you might think.

Help make America strong. "Sell American"... create new jobs... increase profits nationwide ...

Bring Our Money Home Again!

Every time we "sell" an American made product in the international marketplace, those dollars come back into the U.S. economy... increasing profits... creating jobs... making America stronger.

Back when I was 18 years old, I spent over $300 (a lot of money back then) to take a correspondence course in international trade. I worked my buns off studying the course materials, doing the exercises, and passing the tests.

After I finished my correspondence course in international trade, I knocked on doors and beat the bushes until I finally got my first export order from overseas. It wasn't a big order but it was an order.

For three days (and nights), I worked my fingers to the bone preparing all of the forms and documents... just as I had learned in the correspondence course.

With the forms and documents in hand, I loaded the shipment in the pick-up truck and headed to the freight office. Arriving before the office opened, I unloaded my shipment on the dock and waited.

As soon as the freight office opened, I eagerly approached the counter and presented the clerk with all of my completed forms & documents.

Shuffling through my forms, the clerk pulled-out one... just ONE... form from the stack. Using that form, he completed a couple of forms on the counter (in handwriting) and asked me a few questions about the product, price and method of payment

The clerk must have noticed the startled, sick look on my face when he, then, unceremoniously dumped the rest of my forms and documents in the 10-gallon trash can behind the counter. Turning to me with a big grin on his face, he said, "Looks like you took that world trade course, too." Then, he explained the real world to me.

Recently, I received a review copy of an all-new, complete and updated course in international trade.

Guess what? You guessed it! After all these years, they're still teaching the same complex, intricate processing, paperwork jungle, methods I studied when I was 18 years old... and discarded after I made my first real sale overseas.

Is it any wonder that, when someone thinks about getting into international trade, they decide it looks like way too much work.

They're **wrong** but that is part of the attitude that has made this country so weak in the international markets. It seems everybody is "importing" — sending out our money to other countries... instead of "exporting"... to bring money into our economy.

Actually, exporting is even easier than importing... especially today with our government putting more and more emphasis on it.

Besides, as an "importer," you have to "buy" things overseas to sell here... that takes a lot of money. But, as an "exporter," you are "selling" things overseas... which doesn't take much money at all.

As a matter of fact, you can actually start your own export business for a couple hundred dollars. Your very first order could easily return your investment ten-fold (or more).

Beyond that, with from 80% to 85% of U.S. businesses **not** exporting their products, just imagine how many export opportunities exist... even in your own hometown. There are thousands upon thousands of products you can start exporting tomorrow! How?

Well, after I learned that the books and courses on exporting being offered today were no different than the course I took when I was 18 years old, I sat myself down and started putting together notes about how exporting is really done in real world — as opposed to the theoretical textbook world.

Before I knew it, I had written a complete course on exporting that made exporting so simple and easy anyone (I do mean "anyone") can do it. I entitled it, *Sell American.*

Sell American is **not** a correspondence course... or copies of Department of Commerce information... or a textbook... or a doctoral thesis on international trade & economic/political hyperbole. *Sell American* is a "how I did it" and "how you can do it, too" (simple & easy) book, based on my own real life experiences in international trade.

For example, in the book, I tell you the one (and only) form you really need — usually 5 copies — to export almost anything to almost anywhere in the world.

But... if you like to buy information by the pound, you're going to be disappointed. I don't use big words, or fill up pages with complex stuff you will never need to know (just to make the book fat). I just tell you what you need to know to **get the job done.**

That means you won't have to wade through 50 pages of "how to do it" information and later learn you don't have to do it anyway (like I did after taking the correspondence course).

Once you finish reading *Sell American,* you **will** be able to export U.S. made products simply and easily. You will be earning your fortune in the international marketplace. And, at the same time, you will be helping to make America strong by bringing money into our economy from overseas... creating jobs... increasing profits nationwide.

By the way, according to the Department of Commerce, every $45,000 worth of U.S. exports creates a new job in America... **but**... it takes over $90,000 in domestic sales to create that same job.

Sell American is only $99.95... a small price when you consider I paid over 3 times that much for the course I took 30 years ago. Besides, you can easily earn 10 to 20 times that much on your very first export order.

You will learn...

How to Get Started in Exporting

What Products to Export

How To Export Exports, Imports, Used Goods & Closeouts

How & When To Get An Export License

Export Pricing

How To Sell Your Products Overseas

How To Act As An Export Representative

How To Let Your Business Finance Itself

How To Get The Professionals To Do Most Of The Work For You!

You won't need a bunch of money to get started, either, because... **exporting finances itself! Just one export sale can make you a fortune!**

Order your personal copy, **today!**

To order send $104.95 (including $5 shipping and handling) (or Visa, MasterCard, Discover, American Express charge instructions) to:

Phlander Company
Dept. 70197
P. O. Box 5385
Cleveland, Tennessee 37320-5385 U.S.A.
Telephone: +1 706 259-2280
Fax: +1 706 259-2291

About the Author

The eldest son of a farmer/aircraft worker, born in Oklahoma and reared on farms in Oklahoma, Missouri, and Kansas, Straw began his long, successful career in business at the age of nine; when he sold his first cans of Cloverleaf Salve and copies of GRIT newspaper. Even at that early age, he had the unique talent of recognizing an opportunity, implementing a plan, and making a profit.

Straw's career has progressed through direct selling, service contracting, wholesale merchandising, entertainment (he was a professional trumpet player, vocalist & radio announcer), freight forwarding, import/export, retail merchandising, warehousing, real estate, electronics manufacturing, finder's fees, closeout merchandising, financial brokerage, business consulting, steel fabrication, gold & coal mining, offshore banking, mailorder, writing, and publishing.

Over the past 30 years, J.F. Straw has written well over 300 books, booklets, manuals, reports, courses and articles about doing business — all based on his own personal, hands on experience. His writings are "specific& methods, techniques and approaches to doing business that anyone can use to start or expand their business.

As a mailorder marketer...with over 700,000 customers worldwide Straw has sold over $250,000,000 worth of products and services by mail. Everything from Beauty Supplies to Heavy Equipment ... Burglar Alarms to Sleeping Bags... Fishing Lures to Women's Wigs ... Automobiles to Wheelchairs... Investment Opportunities to Seafood ... Consulting Services to "How To" Courses... all by mailorder.

As a member of Mensa, with a lifetime of proven success in marketing, Straw justifiably identifies himself as a "Marketing Genius."

More information on his current products may be obtained on the Internet at http://www.moneyhaven.com/phlander/

APPENDIX

CONTENTS

§ 141.83 Type of invoice required.

(a) [Reserved.]

(b) [Reserved.]

(c) *Commercial invoice.* (1) A commercial invoice shall be filed for each shipment of merchandise not exempted by paragraph (d) of this section. The commercial invoice shall be prepared in the manner customary in the trade, contain the information required by §§ 141.86 through 141.89, and substantiate the statistical information required by § 141.61(e) to be given on the entry, entry summary, or withdrawal documentation.

(2) The port director may accept a copy of a required commercial invoice in place of the original. A copy, other than a photostatic or photographic copy, shall contain a declaration by the foreign seller, the shipper, or the importer that it is a true copy.

(d) *Commercial invoice not required.* A commercial invoice shall not be required in connection with the filing of the entry, entry summary, or withdrawal documentation for merchandise listed in this paragraph. The importer, however, shall present any invoice, memorandum invoice, or bill pertaining to the merchandise which may be in his possession or available to him. If no invoice or bill is available, a pro forma (or substitute) invoice, as provided for in § 141.85, shall be filed, and shall contain information and documentation which verify the information required for statistical purposes by § 141.61(e).

The merchandise subject to the foregoing requirements is as follows:

(1) Merchandise having an aggregate purchase price or value, as specified in paragraph (a) of this section, of $500 or less.

(2) Merchandise not intended for sale or any commercial use in its imported condition or any other form, and not brought in on commission for any person other than the importer.

(3)–(4) [Reserved.]

(5) Merchandise returned to the United States after having been exported for repairs or alteration under subheadings 9802.00.40 and 9802.00.60, Harmonized Tariff Schedule of the United States (19 U.S.C. 1202).

(6) Merchandise shipped abroad, not delivered to the consignee, and returned to the United States.

(7) Merchandise exported from continuous Customs custody within 6 months after the date of entry.

(8) Merchandise consigned to, or entered in the name of, any agency of the U.S. Government.

(9) Merchandise for which an appraisement entry is accepted.

(10) Merchandise entered temporarily into the Customs territory of the United States under bond or for permanent exhibition under bond.

(11) Merchandise provided for in section 466, Tariff Act of 1930 (19 U.S.C. 1466), which pertain to certain equipment, repair parts, and supplies for vessels.

(12) Merchandise imported as supplies, stores, and equipment for the importing carrier and subsequently made subject to entry pursuant to section 446, Tariff Act of 1930, as amended (19 U.S.C. 1446).

(13) Ballast (not including cargo used for ballast) landed from a vessel and delivered for consumption.

(14) Merchandise, whether privileged or nonprivileged, resulting from manipulation or manufacture in a foreign trade zone.

(15) Screenings contained in bulk importations of grain or seeds.

[Treasury Decision (T.D.) 73-175, 38 FR 17447, July 2, 1973, as amended by T.D. 78-53, 43 FR 6069, Feb. 13, 1978; T.D. 79-221, 44 FR 46820, Aug. 9, 1979; T.D. 82-224, 47 FR 53728, Nov. 29, 1982; T.D. 84-213, 49 FR 41184, Oct. 19, 1984; T.D. 85-39, 50 FR 9612, Mar. 11, 1985; T.D. 89-1, 53 FR 51256, Dec. 21, 1988; T.D. 93-66, 58 FR 44130, Aug. 19, 1993; T.D. 94-24, 59 FR 13200, Mar. 21, 1994; T.D. 95-78, 60 FR 50032, Sept. 27, 1995.]

NOTE: *The requirement for special Customs invoice was waived by the Customs Service on March 1, 1982. However, it may still be used. If a commercial invoice is used, it must be signed by the seller and shipper or their agents.*

PRO FORMA INVOICE

Importers Statement of Value or the Price Paid in the Form of an Invoice

Not being in possession of a special or commercial seller's or shipper's invoice I request that you accept the statement of value or the price paid in the form of an invoice submitted below:

Name of shipper _____ address _____

Name of seller _____ address _____

Name of consignee _____ address _____

Name of purchaser _____ address _____

The merchandise (has) (has not) been purchased or agreed to be purchased by me. The prices, or in the case of consigned goods the values, given below are true and correct to the best of my knowledge and belief, and are based upon (check basis with an "X"):

(a) The prices paid or agreed to be paid ( ) as per order dated _____

(b) Advices from exporters by letter ( ) by cable ( ) dated _____

(c) Comparative values of shipments previously received ( ) dated _____

(d) Knowledge of the market in the country of exportation ( )

(e) Knowledge of the market in the United States (if U.S. value) ( )

(f) Advices of the District Director of Customs ( )

(g) Other ( )

A	B	C	D	E	F	G
Case marks numbers	Manufacturer's item number symbol or brand	Quantities and full description	Unit purchase price (currency)	Total purchase price (currency)	Unit foreign value	Total foreign value

Check which of the charges below are, and which are not, included in the prices listed in columns "D" and "E":

Amount Included   Not Included   Amount Included   Not Included

Packing_____

Cartage_____

Inland freight_____

Wharfage and loading
   abroad_____

Country of origin_____

Lighterage_____

Ocean freight_____

U.S. duties_____

Other charges (identify by
   name and amount_____

Total_____

If any other invoice is received, I will immediately file it with the District Director of Customs.

Date _____   Signature of person making invoice _____

                                         Title and firm name _____

2 ADDITIONAL INFORMATION

§ 141.89 Additional Information for certain classes of merchandise.

(a) Invoices for the following classes of merchandise, classifiable under the Harmonized Tariff Schedule of the United States (HTSUS), shall set forth the additional information specified: [T.D. 75-42, 75-239, 78-53, 83-251, 84-149.]

Aluminum and alloys of aluminum classifiable under subheadings 7601.10.60, 7601.20.60, 7601.20.90, or 7602.00.00, HTSUS (T.D. 53092, 55977, 56143)—Statement of the percentages by weight of any metallic element contained in the article.

Articles manufactured of textile materials, Coated or laminated with plastics or rubber, classifiable in Chapter(s) 39, 40, and 42—Include a description indicating whether the fabric is coated or laminated on both sides, on the exterior surface or on the interior surface.

Bags manufactured of plastic sheeting and not of a reinforced or laminated construction, classified in Chapter 39 or in hading 4202—Indicate the gauge of the plastic sheeting.

Ball or roller bearings classifiable under subheading 8482.10.50 through 8482.80.00, HTSUS (T.D. 68-306)—(1) Type of bearing (i.e. whether a ball or roller bearing); (2) If a roller bearing, whether a spherical, tapered, cylindrical, needled or other type; (3) Whether a combination bearing (i.e. a bearing containing both ball and roller bearings, etc.); and (4) If a ball bearing (not including ball bearing with integral shafts or parts of ball bearings), whether or not radial, the following: (a) outside diameter of each bearing; and (b) whether or not a radial bearing (the definition of radial bearing is, for Customs purposes, an antifriction bearing primarily designed to support a load perpendicular to shaft axis).

Beads (T.D. 50088, 55977)—(1) The length of the string, if strung; (2) The size of the beads expressed in millimeters; (3) The material of which the beads are composed, i.e. ivory, glass, imitation pearl, etc.

Bed Linen and Bedspreads—Statement as to whether or not the article contains any embroidery, lace, braid, edging, trimming, piping or applique work.

Chemicals—Furnish the use and Chemical Abstracts Service number of chemical compounds classified in Chapters 27, 28 and 29, HTSUS.

Colors, dyes, stains and related products provided for under heading 3204, HTSUS—The following information is required: (1) Invoice name of product; (2) Trade name of product; (3) Identity and percent by weight of each component; (4) Color Index number (if none, so state); (5) Color Index generic name (if none so state); (6) Chemical Abstracts Service number of the active ingredient; (7) Class of merchandise (state whether acid type dye, basic dye, disperse dye, fluorescent brightener, soluble dye, vat dye, toner or other (describe); (8) Material to which applied (name the material for which the color, dye, or toner is primarily designed).

Copper (T.D. 45878, 50158, 55977) articles classifiable under the provisions of Chapter 74, HTSUS—A statement of the weight of articles of copper, and a statement of percentage of copper content and all other elements—by weight—of articles classifiable according to copper content.

Copper ores and concentrates (T.D. 45878, 50158, 55977) classifiable in heading 2603, and subheadings 2620.19.60, 2620.20.00, 2620.30.00, and heading 7401—Statement of the percentage by weight of the copper content and any other metallic elements.

Cotton fabrics classifiable under the following HTSUS headings: 5208, 5209, 5210, 5211, and 5212—(1) Marks on shipping packages; (2) Numbers on shipping packages; (3) Customer's call number, if any; (4) Exact width of the merchandise; (5) Detailed description of the merchandise; trade name, if any; whether bleached, unbleached, printed, composed of yarns of different color, or dyed; if composed of cotton and other materials, state the percentage of each component material by weight; (6) Number of single threads per square centimeter (All ply yarns must be counted in accordance with the number of single threads contained in the yarn; to illustrate: a cloth containing 100 two-ply yarns in one square centimeter must be reported as 200 single thread); (7) Exact weight per square meter in grams; (8) Average yarn number use this formula:

$$\frac{100 \times (\text{total single yarns per square centimeter})}{(\text{number of grams per square meter})}$$

(9) Yarn size or sizes in the warp; (1) Yarn size or sizes in the filling; (11) Specify whether the yarns are combed or carded; (12) Number of colors or kinds (different yarn sizes or materials) in the filling; (13) Specify whether the fabric is napped or not napped; and (14) Specify the type of weave, for example, plan, twill, sateen, oxford, etc., and (15) Specify the type of machine on which woven: if with Jacquard (Jacq), if with Swivel (Swiv), if with Lappet (Lpt.), if with Dobby (Dobby).

Cotton raw See § 151.82 of this chapter for additional information required on invoices.

Cotton waste (T.D. 50044)—(1) The name by which the cotton waste is known, such as "cotton card strips"; "cotton comber waste"; "cotton fly waste"; etc.; (2) Whether the length of the cotton staple forming any cotton card strips covered by the invoice is less than 3.016 centimeters (1 1/16 inches) or is 3.016 centimeters (1 1/16 inches) or more.

Earthenware or crockeryware composed of a nonvitrified absorbent body (including white granite and semi-porcelain earthenware and cream-colored ware, stoneware, and terra cotta, but not including common brown, gray, red, or yellow earthenware), embossed or plain; common salt-glazed stoneware; stoneware or earthenware crucibles; Rockingham earthenware, china, porcelain, or other vitrified wares, composed of a vitrified nonabsorbent body which, when broken, shows a vitrified, vitreous, semi-vitrified, or semivitreous fracture; and bisque or parian ware (T.D. 53236)—(1) If in sets, the kinds of articles in each set in the shipment and the quantity of each kind of article in each set in the shipment; (2) The exact maximum diameter, expressed in centimeters, of each size of all plates in the shipment; (3) The unit value for each style and size of plate, cup, saucer, or other separate piece in the shipment.

Fish or fish livers (T.D. 50724, 49640, 55977) imported in airtight containers classifiable under Chapter 3, HTSUS—(1) Statement whether the articles contain an oil, fat, or grease, (2) The name and quantity of any such oil, fat, or grease.

Footwear, classifiable in headings 6401 through 6405 of the HTSUS—

1. Manufacturer's style number.

2. Importer's style and/or stock number

3. Percent by area of external surface area of upper (excluding reinforcements and accessories) which is

Leather	a. _____	%
Composition leather	b. _____	%
Rubber and/or plastics	c _____	%
Textile materials	d. _____	%
Other		
(give separate percent for each type of material)	e. _____	%
	f. _____	%

4. Percent by area of external surface area of outersole (excluding reinforcements and accessories) which is:

Leather	a. _____	%
Composition leather	b. _____	%
Rubber and/or plastics	c. _____	%
Textile materials	d. _____	%
Other		
(give separate percent for each type of material)	e _____	%
	f. _____	%

You may skip this section if you choose to answer all questions A through Z below

I.   If 3(a) is larger than any other percent in 3 and if 4(a) is larger than any other percent in 4, answer questions F, G, L, M, O, R, S, and X.

II.   If 3(a) is larger than any other percent in 3 and if 4(c) is larger than any other percent in 4, answer questions F, G, L, M, O, R, S, and X.

III. If 3(a) plus 3(b) is larger than any single percent in 3 and 4(d), 4(e) or 4(f) is larger than any other percent in 4, stop

IV.   If 3(c) is larger than any other percent in 3 and if 4(a) or 4(b) is larger than any other percent in 4, stop

V.   If 3(c) is larger than any other percent in 3 and if 4(c) is larger than any other percent in 4, answer questions B, E, F, G, H, J, K, L, M, N, O, P, T and W

VI.   If 3(d) is larger than any other percent in 3 and if 4(a) plus 4(b) is greater than any single percent in 4, answer questions C and D

VII. If 3(d) is larger than any other percent in 3 and if 4(c) is larger than any single percent in 4, answer questions A, C, J, K, M, N, P and T.

VIII If 3(d) is larger than any other percent in 3 and if 4(d) is larger than any other percent in 4, answer questions U, Y and Z.

IX.   If the article is made of paper, answer questions V and Z.

If the article does not meet any of the conditions I through IX above, answer all questions A through Z, below.

A   Percent of external surface area of upper (including leather reinforcements and accessories).

         Which is leather   _____ %

B   Percent by area of external surface area of upper (including all reinforcements and accessories).

         Which is rubber   _____ %

         and/or plastics   _____ %

C.   Percent by weight of rubber and/or plastics is _____ %

D   Percent by weight of textile materials plus rubber and/or plastics is _____ %

E   Is it waterproof?

F.   Does it have a protective metal toe cap?

G.   Will it cover the wearer's ankle bone?

H.   Will it cover the wearer's knee cap?

I   [Reserved]

J.   Is it designed to be a protection against water, oil, grease, or chemicals or cold or inclement weather?

K.   Is it a slip-on?

L.   Is it a downhill or cross-country ski boot?

M. Is it serious sports footwear other than ski boots? (Chapter 64 subheading note defines sports footwear.)

N. Is it a tennis, basketball, gym, or training shoe or the like?

O. Is it made on a base or platform of wood?

P. Does it have open toes or open heels?

Q. Is it made by the (lipped insole) welt construction?

R. Is it made by the turned construction?

S. Is it worn exclusively by men, boys or youths?

T. Is it made by an exclusively adhesive construction?

U. Are the fibers of the upper, by weight, predominately vegetable fibers?

V. Is it disposable, i.e., intended for one-time use?

W. Is it a "Zori"?

X. Is the leather in the upper pigskin?

Y. Are the sole and supper made of wool felt?

Z. Is there a line of demarcation between the outer sole and upper?

The information requested above may be furnished on CF 5523 or other appropriate format by the exporter, manufacturer or shipper.

Also, the following information must be furnished by the importer or his authorized agent if classification is claimed under one of the subheadings below, as follows:

If subheading 6401.99.80, 6402.19.10, 6402.30.30, 6402.91.40, 6402.99.15, 6402.99.30, 6404.11.40, 6404.11.60, 6404.19.35, 6404.19.40, or 6404.19.60 is claimed:

Does the shoe have a foxing or foxing-like band? If so, state its material(s).

Does the sole overlap the upper other than just at the front of the toe and/or at the back of the heel?

Definitions for some of the terms used in Question A to Z above: For the purpose of this section, the following terms have the approximate definitions below. If either a more complete definition or a decision as to its application to a particular article is needed, the marker or importer of record (or the agent of either) should contact Customs prior to entry of the article.

a. In an **exclusively adhesive construction**, all of the pieces of the bottom would separate from the upper or from each other if all adhesives, cements, and glues were dissolved. It includes shoes in which the pieces of the upper are stitched to each other, but not to any part of the bottom. Examples include:

   1. Vulcanized construction footwear;

   2. Simultaneous molded construction footwear;

   3. Molded footwear in which the upper and the bottom is one piece of molded rubber or plastic, and

   4. Footwear in which staples, rivets, stitching, or any of the methods above are either primary or even just extra or auxiliary, even though adhesive is a major part of the reason the bottom will not separate from the upper.

b. **Composition leather** is made by binding together leather fibers or small pieces of natural leather. It does not include imitation leathers not based on natural leather.

c. **Leather** is the tanned skin of any animal from which the fur or hair has been removed. Tanned skins coated or laminated with rubber and/or plastics are "leather" only if leather gives the material its essential character.

d. A **Line of Demarcation** exists if one can indicate where the sole ends and the upper begins. For example, knit booties do not normally have a line of demarcation.

e. **Men's, boy's and youth's** sizes cover footwear of American youths size 11 and larger for males, and does not include footwear commonly worn by both sexes. If more than 4% of the shoes sold in a given size will be worn by females, that size is "commonly worn by both sexes."

f. Footwear is designed to *protect* against water, oil or cold or inclement weather only if it is substantially more of a protection against those items than the usual shoes of that type. For example, a leather oxford will clearly keep your feet warmer and drier than going barefoot, but they are not a protection in this sense. On the other hand, the snow-jogger is the protective version of the nonprotective jogging shoe.

g. **Rubber and/or plastics** includes any textile material visibly coated (or covered) externally with one or both of those materials.

h. **Slip-on** includes:

   1. A boot which must be pulled on.

   2. Footwear with elastic cores which must be stretched to get it on, but not a separate piece of elasticized fabric which forms a full circle around the foot or ankle.

i. **Sports footwear** includes only:

   1. Footwear which is designed for a sporting activity and has, or has provision for, the attachment of spikes, sprigs, cleats, stops, clips, bars or the like;

   2. Skating boots (without skates attached), ski boots and cross-country ski footwear, wrestling boots, boxing boots and cycling shoes.

j. **Tennis shoes, basketball shoes, gym shoes, training shoes and the like** cover athletic footwear other than sports footwear, whether or not principally used for such athletic games or purposes.

k. **Textile materials** are made from cotton, other vegetable fibers, wool, hair, silk or man-made fibers. Note: Cork, wood, cardboard and leather are not textile materials.

l. In **turned** construction, the upper is stitched to the leather sole wrong side out and the shoe is then turned right side out.

m. **Vegetable fibers** include cotton, flax and ramie, but does not include either rayon or plaiting materials such as rattan or wood strips.

n. **Waterproof footwear** includes footwear designed to protect against penetration by water or other liquids, whether or not such footwear is primarily designed for such purposes.

o. **Welt footwear** means footwear construction with a welt, which extends around the edge of the outer sole, and in which the welt and shoe upper are sewed to a lip on the surface of the insole, and the outer sole of which is sewed or cemented to the welt.

p. A **zori** has an upper consisting only of straps or thongs of molded rubber or plastic. This upper is assembled to a formed rubber or plastic sole by means of plugs.

Fur products and furs (T.D. 53064)—(1) Name or names (as set forth in the Fur Products Name Guide (16 CFR 301.0) of the animal or animals that produced the fur, and such qualifying statements as may be required pursuant to § 7(c) of the Fur Products Labeling Act (15 U.S.C. 69e(c)); (2) A statement that the fur product contains or is composed of used fur, when such is the fact; (3) A statement that the fur product contains or is composed of bleached, dyed, or otherwise artificially colored fur, when such is the fact; (4) A statement that the fur product is composed in whole or in substantial part of paws, tails, bellies, or waste fur, when such is the fact, (5) Name and address of the manufacturer of the fur product; (6) Name of the country of origin of the furs or those contained in the fur product.

Glassware and other glass products (T.D. 53079, 55977)—Classifiable under Chapter 70, HTSUS—Statement of the separate value of each component article in the set.

Gloves—classifiable in subheadings 6116.10.20 and 6216.00.20—Statement as to whether or not the article has been covered with plastics on both sides.

Grain or grain and screenings (T.D. 51284)—Statement on Customs invoices for cultivated grain or grain and screenings that no screenings are included with the grain, or, if there are screenings included, the percentage of the shipment which consists of screenings commingled with the principal grain.

Handkerchiefs—(1) State the exact dimensions (length and width) of the merchandise; (2) If of cotton indicate whether the handkerchief is hemmed and whether it contains lace or embroidery.

Hats or headgear—(1) If classifiable under subheading 6502.00.40 or 6502.00.60, HTSUS—Statement as to whether or not the article has been bleached or colored; (2) If classifiable under subheading 6502.00.20 through 6502.00.60 or 6504.00.30 through 6504.00.90, HTSUS—Statement as to whether or not the article is sewed or not sewed, exclusive of any ornamentation or trimming.

Hosiery—(1) Indicate whether a single yarn measures less than 67 decitex. (2) Indicate whether the hosiery is full length, knee length, or less than knee length. (3) Indicate whether it contains lace or net.

Iron or Steel classifiable in Chapter 72 or headings 7301 to 7307, HTSUS (T.D. 53092, 55977)—Statement of the percentages by weight of carbon and any metallic elements contained in the articles, in the form of a mill analysis or mill test certificate.

Iron oxide (T.D. 49989, 50107)—For iron oxide to which a reduced rate of duty is applicable, a statement of the method of preparation of the oxide, together with the patent number, if any.

Machines, equipment and apparatus—Chapters 84 and 85, HTSUS—A statement as to the use or method of operation of each type of machine.

Machine parts (T.D. 51616)—Statement specifying the kind of machine for which the parts are intended, or if this is not known to the shipper, the kinds of machines for which the parts are suitable.

Machine tools: (1) Heading 8456 through 8462—machine tools covered by these headings equipped with a CNC (Computer Numerical Control) or the facings (electrical interface) for a CNC must state so; (2) heading 8458 through 8463—machine tools covered by these headings if used or rebuilt must state so; (3) subheading 8456.30 10—EDM. (Electrical Discharge Machines) if a Traveling Wire (Wire Cut) type must state so. Wire EDM's use a copper or brass wire for the electrode; (4) subheading 8457.10.0010 through 8457.10.0050—Machining Centers. Must state whether or not they have an ATC (Automatic Tool Changer). Vertical spindle machine centers with an ATC must also indicate the Y-travel; (5) subheadings 8458.11.0030 through 8458.11.00.90—horizontal lathes: numerically controlled. Must indicate the rated HP (or KW rating) of the main spindle motor. Use the continuous rather than 30-minute rating.

Madeira embroideries (T.D. 49988)—(1) With respect to the materials used, furnish: (a) country of production; (b) width of the material in the piece; (c) name of the manufacturer; (d) kind of material, indicating manufacturer's quality number; (e) landed cost of the material used in each item; (f) date of the order; (g) date of the invoice; (h) invoice unit value in the currency of the purchase; (i) discount from purchase price allowed, if any, (2) with respect to the finished embroidered articles, furnish: (a) manufacturer's name, design number, and quality number; (b) importer's design number, if any; (c) finished size; (d) number of embroidery points per unit of quantity; (e) total for overhead and profit added in arriving at the price of value of the merchandise covered by the invoice.

Motion-picture films—(1) Statement of footage, title, and subject matter of each film; (2) declaration of shipper, cameraman, or other person with knowledge of the acts identifying the films with the invoice and stating that the basic films were to the best of his knowledge and belief exposed abroad and returned for use as newsreel; (3) declaration of importer that he believes the films entered by him are the ones covered by the preceding declaration and that the films are intended for use as newsreel.

Paper classifiable in Chapter 48—Invoices covering paper shall contain the following information, or will be accompanied by specification sheets containing such information:

(1) weight of paper in grams per square meter; (2) thickness, in micrometers (microns); (3) if imported in rectangular sheets, length and width sheets, in cm; (4) if imported in strips, or rolls, the width, in cm. In the case of rolls, the diameter of rolls in cm; (5) whether the paper is coated or impregnated, and with what materials; (6) weight of coating, in grams per square meter; (7) percentage by weight of the total fiber content consisting of wood fibers contained by a mechanical process, chemical sulfate or soda process, chemical sulfite process, or semi-chemical process, as appropriate; (8) commercial designation, as "writing", "cover", "drawing", "Bristol", "newsprint", etc.; (9) ash content; (10) color; (11) glaze, or finish; (12) Mullen bursting strength, and Mullen index; (13) stretch factor, in machine direction and in cross direction; (14) tear and tensile readings; in machine direction, in cross direction, and in machine direction plus cross direction; (15) identification of fibers as "hardwood" where appropriate; (16) crush resistance; (17) brightness; (18) smoothness; (19) if bleached, whether bleached uniformly throughout the mass; (20) whether embossed, perforated, creped or crinkled.

Plastic plates, sheets, film, foil and strip of headings 3920 and 3921—(1) Statement as to whether the plastic is cellular or noncellular; (2) specification of the type of plastic: (3) indication of whether or not flexible and whether combined with textile or other material.

Printed matter classifiable in Chapter 49—Printed matter entered in the following headings shall have, on or with the invoices covering such matter, the following information: (1) Heading 4901—(a) whether the books are: dictionaries, encyclopedias, textbooks, bound newspapers or journals or periodicals, directories, bibles or other prayer books, technical, scientific or professional books, art or pictorial books, or "other" books; (b) if "other" books, whether hardbound or paperbound; (c) if "other" books, paperbound, other than "rack size": number of pages (excluding covers). (2) Heading 4902—(a) whether the journal or periodical appears at least four times a week. If the journal or periodical appears other than at least four times a week, whether it is a newspaper supplement printed by a gravure process, is a newspaper, busi-

ness or professional journal or periodical, or other than these; (3) Heading 4904—whether the printed or manuscript music is sheet music, not bound (except by stapling or folding); (4) Heading 4905—(a) whether globes, or not; (b) if not globes, whether in book form, or not; (c) in any case, whether or not in relief; (5) Heading 4908—Whether or not vitrifiable; (6) Heading 4904—whether post cards, greeting cards, or other; (7) Heading 4910—(a) whether or not printed on paper by a lithographic process; (b) if printed on paper by a lithographic process, the thickness of the paper, in mum; (8) Subheading 4911.91—(a) whether or not printed over 20 years at time of importation; (b) if not printed over 20 years at time of importation, whether suitable for use in the production of articles of heading 4902; (c) if not printed over 20 years at time of importation, and not suitable for use in the production of articles of heading 4901, whether the merchandise is lithographs on paper or paperboard; (d) if lithographs on paper or paperboard, under the terms of the immediately preceding description, thickness of the paper or paperboard, and whether or not posters; (e) in any case, whether or not posters; (f) in any case, whether or not photographic negatives or positives on transparent bases; (b) Subheading 4911.99—If not carnets, or parts thereof, in English or French, whether or not printed on paper in whole or in part by a lithographic process.

Pulp classifiable in Chapter 47—(1) Invoices covering chemical woodpulp, dissolving trades, in Heading 4702 shall state the insoluble fraction (as percentage) after 1 hour in a caustic soda solution containing 18% sodium hydroxide (NaOH) at 20o C; (2) Subheading 4702.00.0020—Pulp entered under this subheading shall in addition contain on or with the invoice the ash content as a percentage by weight.

Refrigeration equipment (1) Refrigerator-freezers classifiable under subheading 8418.10.00 and (2) refrigerators classifiable under 8418.21.00—(a) statement as to whether they are compression or absorption type; (b) statement of other refrigerated volume in liters; (3) freezers classifiable under subheading 8418.30.00 and 8418.40.00—statement as to whether they are chest or upright type; (4) liquid chilling refrigerating unless classifiable under subheading 8418.69.0045 through 8418.69.0060—statement as to whether they are centrifugal open-type, centrifugal hermetic-type, absorption-type or reciprocating type.

Rolling mills—Subheading 8455.30.0005 through 8455.30.0085. Rolls for rolling mills: Indicate the composition of the roll—gray iron, cast steel or other—and the weight of each roll.

Rubber Products of Chapter 40—(1) Statement as to whether combined with textile or other material; (2) statement whether the rubber is cellular or noncellular, unvulcanized or vulcanized, and if vulcanized, whether hard rubber or other than hard rubber.

Screenings or scalpings of grains or seeds (T.D. 51096)—(1) Whether the commodity is the product of a screening process; (2) if so, whether any cultivated grains have been added to such commodity; (3) If any such grains have been added, the kind and percentage of each.

Textile fiber products (T.D. 55095—(1) The constituent fiber or combination of fibers in the textile fiber product, designating with equal prominence each natural or manufactured fiber in the textile fiber product by its generic name in the order of predominance by the weight thereof if the weight of such fiber is 5 percent or more of the total fiber weight of the product; (2) percentage of each fiber present, by weight, in the total fiber content of the textile fiber product; (3) the name, or other identification issued and registered by the Federal Trade Commission, of the manufacturer of the product or one or more persons subject to § 3 of the Textile Fiber Products Identification Act (15 U.S.C. 70a) with respect to such product; (4) the name of the country where processed or manufactured. See also "Wearing Apparel" below.

Tires and Tubes for tires, of rubber or plastics—(1) Specify the kind of vehicle for which the tire is intended, i.e. airplane, bicycle, passenger car, on-the-highway light or heavy truck or bus, motorcycle; (2) if designed for tractors provided for in subheading 8701 90.10, or for agricultural or horticultural machinery or implements provided for in Chapter 84 or in subheading 8716.80.10, designate whether the tire is new, recapped, or used; pneumatic or solid; (3) indicate whether the tube is designed for tires provided for in subheading 4011.91.10, 4011.99.10, 4012.10.20, or 4012.20.20.

Tobacco (including tobacco in its natural state) (T.D. 44854, 45871)—(1) Specify in detail the character of the tobacco in each bale by giving (a) country and province of origin, (b) year of production, (c) grade or grades in each bale, (d) number of carrots or pounds of each grade if more than one grade is packed in a bale, (e) the time when, place where, and person from whom purchased, (f) price paid or to be paid for each bale or package, or price for the vega or lot is purchased in bulk, or if obtained otherwise than by purchase, state the actual market value per bale; (2) if an invoice covers or includes bales of tobacco which are part of a vega or lot purchased in bulk, the invoice must contain or be accompanied by a full description of the vega or lot purchased; or if such description has been furnished with a previous importation, the date and identity of such shipment; (3) packages or bales containing only filler leaf shall be invoiced as filler; when containing filler and wrapper but not more than 35 percent of wrapper, they shall be invoiced as mixed; and when containing more than 35 percent of wrapper, they shall be invoiced as wrapper.

Watches and watch movements classifiable under Chapter 91 of the HTSUS—For all commercial shipments of such articles, there shall be required to be shown on the invoice, or on a separate sheet attached to and constituting a part of the invoice, such information as will reflect with respect to each group, type, or model, the following:

(A) For watches, a thorough description of the composition of the watch cases, the bracelets, bands or straps, the commercial description (ebauche caliber number, ligne size and number of jewels) of the movements contained in the watches, and the type of battery (manufacturer's name and reference number), if the watch is battery operated.

(B) For watch movements, the commercial description (ebauche caliber number, ligne size and number of jewels). If battery-operated, the type of battery (manufacturer's name and reference number).

(C) The name of the manufacturer of the exported watch movements and the name of the country in which the movements were manufactured.

Wearing apparel—(a) All invoices for textile wearing apparel should indicate a component material breakdown in percentages by weight for all component fibers present in the entire garment, as well as separate breakdowns of the fibers in the (outer) shell (exclusive of linings, cuffs, waistbands, collars and other trimmings) and in the lining; (2) for garments which are constructed of more than one component or material (combination of knits and not knit fabric or combinations of knit and/or not knit fabric with leather, fur, plastic including vinyl, etc.), the invoice must show a fiber breakdown in percentages by weight for each separate textile material in the garment and a breakdown in percentages by weight for each nontextile material for the entire garment; (3) for woven garments-indicate whether the fabric is yarn dyed and whether there are "two or more colors in the warp and/or filling"; (4) for all-white T-shirts and singlets Indicate whether or not the garment contains pockets, trim, or embroidery; (5) for mufflers-State the exact dimensions (length and width) of the merchandise.

Wood products—(1) Wood sawed or chipped lengthwise, sliced or peeled, whether or not planed, sanded, or finger-jointed, of a thickness exceeding 6 mm (lumber), classifiable under Chapter 44 heading 4407, HTSUS, and wood continuously shaped along any of its edges or faces, whether or not planed, sanded or finger-jointed; coniferous: Subheading 4409.10.90 and nonconiferous: Subheading 4409.20.90, HTSUS, and dutiable on the basis of cubic meters—

Quantity in cubic meter (m) before dressing; (2) fiberboard of wood or other ligneous materials whether or not bonded with resins or other organic substances, under Chapter 44, Heading 4411, HTSUS, and classifiable according to its density-

density in grams per cubic centimeter (cm); (3) plywood consisting solely of sheets of wood, classifiable under Chapter 44, Subheading 4412.11,4412.12, and 4412.19, HTSUS, and classifiable according to the thickness of the wood sheets-thickness of each ply in millimeter (mm);

Wool and hair—See 151.62 of this chapter for additional information required on invoices.

Wool products, except carpets, rugs, mats, and upholsteries, and wool products made more than 20 years before importation (T.D. 50388, 51019) (1) The percentage of the total fiber weight of the wool product, exclusive of ornamentation not exceeding 5 per cent of said total fiber weight, of (a) wool; (b) reprocessed wool; (c) reused wool; (d) each fiber other than wool if said percentage by weight of such fiber is 5 per cent or more; and (e) the aggregate of all fibers; (2) the maximum percentage of the total weight of the wool product, of any nonfibrous loading, filling, or adulterating matter; and (3) the name of the manufacturer of the wool product, except when such product consists of mixed wastes, residues, and similar merchandise obtained from several suppliers or unknown sources.

Woven fabric of man-made fibers in headings 5407, 5408, 5512, 5513, 5514, 5515, 5516—

(1) State the exact width of the fabric.

(2) Provide a detailed description of the merchandise, (trade name, if any).

(3) Indicate whether bleached, unbleached, dyed, or yarns of different colors and/or printed.

(4) If composed of more than one material, list percentage by weight in each.

(5) Identify the man-made fibers as artificial or synthetic, filament or staple, and state whether the yarns are high tenacity. Specify the number of turns per meter in each yarn.

(6) Specify yarn sizes in warp and filling.

(7) Specify how the fabric is woven (plain weave, twill, sateen, dobby, jacquard, swivel, lappet, etc.)

(8) Indicate the number of single threads per square centimeter in both warp and filling.

(9) Supply the weight per square meter in grams.

10) Provide the average yarn number using this formula:

100 x number of single threads per square centimeter

(number of grams per square meter)

(11) For spun yarns, specify whether textured or not textured.

(12) For filament yarns, specify whether textured or not textured.

Yarns—(1) All yarn invoices should show: (a) fiber content by weight; (b) whether single or plied; (c) whether or not put up for retail sale (See Section XI, Note 4, HTSUS);

    (d) whether or not intended for use as sewing thread.

(2) If chief weight of silk, show whether spun or filament.

(3) If chief weight of cotton, show:

    (a) whether combed or uncombed

    (b) metric number (mn)

    (c) whether bleached and/or mercerized.

(4) If chief weight of man-made fiber, show:

    (a) whether filament, or spun, or a combination of filament and spun

    (b) If a combination of filament and spun-give percent age of filament and spun by weight.

(5) If chief weight of filament man-made fiber, show:

    (a) whether high tenacity (See Section XI, note 6 HTSUS)

    (b) whether monofilament, multifilament or strip

    (c) whether texturized

    (d) yarn number in decitex

    (e) number of turns per meter

    (f) for monofilaments-show cross-sectional dimension in millimeters

    (g) for strips, show the width of the strip in millimeters (measure in folded or twisted condition if so imported)

Items or classes of goods may be added to or removed from the list from time to time.

3. CUSTOMS VALUATION

93 STAT. 194 PUBLIC LAW 96-39—JULY 26, 1979

TARIFF ACT OF 1930

"SEC 402, VALUE [19 U S C. 1401a]

"(a) IN GENERAL —(1) Except as otherwise specifically provided for in this Act, imported merchandise shall be appraised, for the purposes of this Act, on the basis of the following·

"(A) The transaction value provided for under subsection (b)

"(B) The transaction value of identical merchandise provided for under subsection (c), if the value referred to in subparagraph (A) cannot be determined, or can be determined but cannot be used by reason of subsection (b)(2).

"(C) The transaction value of similar merchandise provided or under subsection (c), if the value referred to in subparagraph (B) cannot be determined

"(D) The deductive value provided for under subsection (d), if the value referred to in subparagraph (C) cannot be determined and if the importer does not request alternative valuation under Paragraph (2).

"(E) The computed value provided for under subsection (e), if the value referred to in subparagraph (D) cannot be determined

"(F) The value provided for under subsection (f), if the value referred to in subparagraph (E) cannot be determined

"(2) If the value referred to in paragraph (1)(C) cannot be determined with respect to imported merchandise, the merchandise shall be appraised on the basis of the computed value provided for under paragraph (1)(E), rather than the deductive value provided for under paragraph (1)(D), if the importer makes a request to that effect to the customs officer concerned within such time as the Secretary shall prescribe If the computed value of the merchandise cannot subsequently be determined, the merchandise may not be appraised on the basis of the value referred to in paragraph (1)(F) unless the deductive value of the merchandise cannot be determined under paragraph (1)(D)

"(3) Upon written request therefor by the importer of merchandise, and subject to provisions of law regarding the disclosure of information, the customs officer concerned shall provide the importer with a written explanation of how the value of that merchandise was determined under this section

"(b) TRANSACTION VALUE OF IMPORTED MERCHANDISE.-(1) The transaction value of imported merchandise is the price actually paid or payable for the merchandise when sold for exportation to the United States, plus amounts equal to—

"(A) the packing costs incurred by the buyer with respect to the imported merchandise;

"(B) any selling commission incurred by the buyer with respect to the imported merchandise;

"(C) the value, apportioned as appropriate, of any assist;

"(D) any royalty or license fee related to the imported merchandise that the buyer is required to pay directly or indirectly, as a condition of the sale of the imported merchandise for exportation to the United States, and

"(E) the proceeds of any subsequent resale, disposal, or use of the imported merchandise that accrue, directly or indirectly, to the seller.

The price actually paid or payable for imported merchandise shall be increased by the amounts attributable to the items (and no others) described in subparagraphs (A) through (E) only to the extent that each such amount (i) is not otherwise included within the price actually paid or payable, and (ii) is based on sufficient information. If sufficient information is not available, for any reason, with respect to any amount referred to in the preceding sentence, the transaction value of the imported merchandise concerned shall be treated, for purposes of this section, as one that cannot be determined.

"(2)(A) The transaction value of imported merchandise determined under paragraph (1) shall be the appraised value of that merchandise for the purposes of this Act only if—

"(i) there are no restrictions on the disposition or use of the imported merchandise by the buyer other than restrictions that—

"(I) are imposed or required by law,

"(II) limit the geographical area in which the merchandise may be resold, or

"(III) do not substantially affect the value of the merchandise,

"(ii) the sale of, or the price actually paid or payable for, the imported merchandise is not subject to any condition or consideration for which a value cannot be determined with respect to the imported merchandise;

"(iii) no part of the proceeds of any subsequent resale, disposal, or use of the imported merchandise by the buyer will accrue directly or indirectly to the seller, unless an appropriate adjustment therefor can be made under paragraph (1)(E); and

"(iv) the buyer and seller are not related, or the buyer and seller are related but the transaction value is acceptable, for purposes of this subsection, under subparagraph (B).

"(B) The transaction value between a related buyer and seller is acceptable for the purposes of this subsection if an examination of the circumstances of the sale of the imported merchandise indicates that the relationship between such buyer and seller did not influence the price actually paid or payable; or if the transaction value of the imported merchandise closely approximates—

Amended by.P.L. 96—490, effective 1/1/81:

"(i) the transaction value of identical merchandise, or of similar merchandise in sales to unrelated buyers in the United States; or

"(ii) the deductive value or computed value for identical merchandise or similar merchandise; but, only if each value referred to in clause (i) or (ii) that is used for comparison relates to merchandise that was exported to the United States at or about the same time as the imported merchandise

"(C) In applying the values used for comparison purposes under subparagraph (B), there shall be taken into account differences with respect to the sales involved (if such differences are based on sufficient information whether supplied by the buyer or otherwise available to the customs officer concerned) in—

"(i) commercial levels;

"(ii) quantity levels;

"(iii) the costs commissions, values, fees, and proceeds described in paragraph (1); and

"(iv) the costs incurred by the seller in sales in which he and the buyer are not related that are not incurred by the seller in sales in which he and the buyer are related.

"(3) The transaction value of imported merchandise does not include any of the following, if identified separately from the price actually paid or payable and from any cost or other item referred to in paragraph (1):

"(A) Any reasonable cost or charge that is incurred for—

(i) the construction, erection, assembly, or maintenance of, or the technical assistance provided with respect to, the merchandise after its importation into the United States; or

"(ii) the transportation of the merchandise after such importation.

"(B) The customs duties and other Federal taxes currently payable on the imported merchandise by reason of its importation, and any Federal excise tax on, or measured by the value of, such merchandise for which vendors in the United States are ordinarily liable.

"(4) For purposes of this subsection—

Price Actually Paid or Payable:

"(A) The term 'price actually paid or payable' means the total payment (whether direct or indirect, and exclusive of any costs, charges, or expenses incurred for transportation, insurance, and related services incident to the international shipment of the merchandise from the country of exportation to the place of importation in the United States) made, or to be made, for imported merchandise by the buyer to, or for the benefit of, the seller.

"(B) Any rebate of, or other decrease in, the price actually paid or payable that is made or otherwise effected between the buyer and seller after the date of the importation of the merchandise into the United

States shall be disregarded in determining the transaction value under paragraph (1).

"(C), TRANSACTION VALUE OF IDENTICAL MERCHANDISE AND SIMILAR MERCHANDISE.—(1) The t,transaction value of identical merchandise, or of similar merchandise, is the transaction value (acceptable as the appraised value for purposes of this Act under subsection (b) but adjusted under paragraph (2) of this subsection) of imported merchandise that is—

"(A) with respect to the merchandise being appraised, either identical merchandise or similar merchandise, as the case may be; and

"(B) exported to the United States at or about the time that the merchandise being appraised is exported to the United States.

"(2) Transaction values determined under this subsection shall be based on sales of identical merchandise or similar merchandise, as the case may be, at the same commercial level and in substantially the same quantity as the sales of the merchandise being appraised. If no such sale is found, sales of identical merchandise or similar merchandise at either a different commercial level or in different quantities, or both, shall be used, but adjusted to take account of any such difference. Any adjustment made under this paragraph shall be based on sufficient information. If in applying this paragraph with respect to any imported merchandise, two or more transaction values for identical merchandise, or for similar merchandise, are determined, such imported merchandise shall be appraised on the basis of the lower or lowest of such values.

Merchandise concerned

"(d) DEDUCTIVE VALUE.—(1) For purposes of this subsection, the term 'merchandise concerned' means the merchandise being appraised, identical merchandise, or similar merchandise.

"(2)(A) The deductive value of the merchandise being appraised is whichever of the following prices (as adjusted under paragraph (3)) is appropriate depending upon when and in what condition the merchandise concerned is sold in the United States:

"(i) if the merchandise concerned is sold in the condition as imported at or about the date of importation of the merchandise being appraised, the price is the unit price at which the merchandise concerned is sold in the greatest aggregate quantity at or about such date.

"(ii) If the merchandise concerned is sold in the condition as imported but not sold at or about the date of importation of the merchandise being appraised, the price is the unit price at which the merchandise concerned is sold in the greatest aggregate quantity after the date of importation of the merchandise being appraised but before the close of the 90th day after the date of such importation.

"(iii) If the merchandise concerned was not sold in the condition as imported and not sold before the close of the 90th day after the date of importation of the merchandise being appraised, the price is the unit price at which the merchandise being appraised, after further processing, is sold in the greatest aggregate quantity before the 180th day after the date of such importation. This clause shall apply to appraisement of merchandise only if the importer so elects and notifies the customs officer concerned of that election within such time as shall be prescribed by the Secretary.

Unit Price

"(B) For purposes of subparagraph (A), the unit price at which merchandise is sold in the greatest aggregate quantity is the unit price at which such merchandise is sold to unrelated persons, at the first commercial level after importation (in cases to which subparagraph (A)(iii) applies) at which such sales take place, in a total volume that is (i) greater than the total volume sold at any other unit price, and (ii) sufficient to establish the unit price.

"(3)(A) The price determined under paragraph (2) shall be reduced by an amount equal to—

"(i) any commission usually paid or agreed to be paid, or the addition usually made for profit and general expenses, in connection with sales in the United States of imported merchandise that is of the same class or kind, regardless of the country of exportation as the merchandise concerned;

"(ii) the actual costs and associated costs of transportation and insurance incurred with respect to international shipments of the merchandise concerned from the country of exportation to the United States;

"(iii) the usual costs and associated costs of transportation and insurance incurred with respect to shipments of such merchandise from the place of importation to the place of delivery in the United States, if such costs are not included as a general expense under clause (i);

"(iv) the customs duties and other Federal taxes currently payable on the merchandise concerned by reason of its importation, and any Federal excise tax on, or measured by the value of, such merchandise for which vendors in the United States are ordinarily liable: and

"(v) (but only in the case of a price determined under paragraph (2)(A)(iii)) the value added by the processing of the merchandise after importation to the extent that the value is based on sufficient information relating to cost of such processing.

"(B) For purposes of applying paragraph (A)—

"(i) the deduction made for profits and general expenses shall be based upon the importer's profits and general expenses, unless such profits and general expenses are inconsistent with those reflected in sales in the United States of imported merchandise of the same class or kind, in which case the deduction shall be based on the usual profit and general expenses reflected in such sales, as determined from sufficient information; and

"(ii) any State or local tax imposed on the importer with respect to the sale of imported merchandise shall be treated as a general expense.

"(C) The price determined under paragraph (2) shall be increased (but only to the extent that such costs are not otherwise included) by an amount equal to the pack-ing costs incurred by the importer or the buyer, as the case may be, with respect to the merchandise concerned.

"(D) For purposes of determining the deductive value of imported merchandise, any sale to a person who supplies any assist for use in connection with the production or sale for export of the merchandise concerned shall be disregarded.

"(e) COMPUTED VALUE.—(1) The computed value of imported merchandise is the sum of—

"(A) the cost or value of the materials and the fabrication and other processing of any kind employed in the production of the imported merchandise

"(B) an amount for profit and general expenses equal to that usually reflected in sales of merchandise of the same class or kind as the imported merchandise that are made by the producers in the country of exportation for export to the United States;

"(C) any assist, if its value is not included under subparagraph (A) or (B); and

"(D) the packing costs

"(2) For purposes of paragraph (1)—

"(A) the cost or value of materials under paragraph (1)(A) shall not include the amount of any internal tax imposed by the country of exportation that is directly applicable to the materials or their disposition if the tax is remitted or refunded upon the exportation of the merchandise in the production of which the materials were used; and

"(B) the amount for profit and general expenses under paragraph (1)(B) shall be used upon the producer's profits and expenses, unless the producer's profits and expenses are inconsistent with those usually reflected in sales of merchandise of the same class or kind as the imported merchandise that are made by producers in the country of exportation for export to the United States, in which case the amount under paragraph (1)(B) shall be used on the usual profit and general expenses of such producers in such sales, as determined from sufficient information.

"(f) VALUE IF OTHER VALUES CANNOT BE DETERMINED OR USED.—(1) If the value of imported merchandise cannot be determined, or otherwise used for the purposes of this Act, under subsections (b) through (e), the merchandise shall be appraised for the purposes of this Act on the basis of a value that is derived from the methods set forth in such subsections, with such methods being reasonably adjusted to the extent necessary to arrive at a value.

Imported Merchandise Appraisal:

"(2) Imported merchandise may not be appraised, for the purposes of this Act, on the basis of—

"(A) the selling price in the United States of merchandise produced in the United States;

"(B) a system that provides for the appraisement of imported merchandise at the higher of two alternative values

"(C) the price of merchandise in the domestic market of the country of exportation

"(D) a cost of production, other than a value determined under subsection (c) for merchandise that is identical merchandise or similar merchandise to the merchandise being appraised;

"(E) the price of merchandise for export to a country other than the United States;

"(F) minimum values for appraisement; or

"(G) arbitrary or fictitious values.

This paragraph shall not apply with respect to the ascertainment, determination, or estimation of foreign market value or United States price under title VII.

Ante, p. 150.

"(g) SPECIAL RULES—(1) for purposes of this section, the persons specified in any of the following subparagraphs shall be treated as persons who are related:

"(A) Members of the same family, including brothers and sisters (whether by whole or half blood), spouse, ancestors, and lineal descendants.

"(B) Any officer or director of an organization and such organization.

"(C) Any officer or director of an organization and an officer or director of another organization, if each such individual is also an officer or director in the other organization.

"(D) Partners.

"(D) Employer and employee.

"(F) Any person directly or indirectly owning, controlling, or holding with power to vote, 5 percent or more of the outstanding voting stock or shares of any organization and such organization.

"(G) Two or more persons directly or indirectly controlling, controlled by, or under common control with, any person.

"(2) For purposes of this section, merchandise (including, but not limited to, identical merchandise and similar merchandise) shall be treated as being of the same class or kind as other merchandise if it is within a group or range of merchandise produced by a particular industry or industry sector.

Generally Accepted Accounting Principles:

"(3) For purposes of this section, information that is submitted by an importer, buyer, or producer in regard to the appraisement of merchandise may not be rejected by the customs officer concerned on the basis of the accounting method by which that information was prepared, if the preparation was in accordance with generally accepted accounting principles. The term generally accepted accounting principles' refers to any generally recognized consensus or substantial authoritative support regarding—

"(A) which economic resources and obligations should be recorded as assets and liabilities;

"(B) which changes in assets and liabilities should be recorded,

"(C) how the assets and liabilities and changes in them should be measured;

"(D) what information should be disclosed and how it should be disclosed; and

"(E) which financial statements should be prepared.

The applicability of a particular set of generally accepted accounting principles will depend upon the basis on which the value of the merchandise is sought to be established.

"(h) DEFINITIONS.—As used in this section—

"(1)(A) The term 'assist' means any of the following if supplied directly or indirectly, and free of charge or at reduced cost, by the buyer of imported merchandise for use in connection with the production or the sale for export to the United States of the merchandise:

"(i) Materials, components, parts and similar items incorporated in the imported merchandise.

"(ii) Tools, dies, molds, and similar items used in the production of the imported merchandise.

"(iii) Merchandise consumed in the production of the imported merchandise.

"(iv) Engineering, development, artwork, design work, and plans and sketches that are undertaken elsewhere than in the United States and are necessary for the production of the imported merchandise.

"(B) No service or work to which subparagraph (A)(iv) applies shall be treated as an assist for purposes of this section if such service or work—

"(i) is performed by an individual who is domiciled with the United States;

"(ii) is performed by that individual while he is acting as an employee or agent of the buyer of the imported merchandise; and

"(iii) is incidental to other engineering, development, artwork, design work, or plans or sketches that are undertaken within the United States.

"(C) For purposes of this section, the following apply in determining the value of assists described in subparagraph (A)(iv):

"(i) The value of an assist that is available in the public domain is the cost of obtaining copies of the assist,

"(ii) If the production of an assist occurred in the United States and one or more foreign countries, the value of the assist is the value thereof that is added outside the United States.

"(2) The term 'identical merchandise' means—

"(A) merchandise that is identical in all respects to, and was produced in the same country and by the same person as, the merchandise being appraised; or

"(B) if merchandise meeting the requirements under subparagraph (A) cannot be found (or for purposes of applying subsection (b)(2)(B)(i), regardless of whether merchandise meeting such requirements can.be found), merchandise that is identical in all respect to, and was produced in the same country as, but not produced by the same person as, the merchandise being appraised.

Such term does not include merchandise that incorporates or reflect any engineering, development, artwork, design work, or plan or sketch that—

"(I) was supplied free or at reduced cost by the buyer or the merchandise for use in connection with the production or the sale for export to the United States of the merchandise; and

"(II) is not an assist because undertaken with the United States

"(3) The term 'packing costs' means the cost of all containers and coverings of whether nature and of packing, whether for labor or materials, used in placing merchandise in condition, packed ready for shipment to the United States

"(4) The term 'similar merchandise' means—

"(A) merchandise that—

"(i) was produced in the same country and by the same person as the merchandise being appraised,

"(ii) is like the merchandise being appraised in characteristics and component material, and

"(iii) is commercially interchangeable with the merchandise being appraised; or

"(B) if merchandise meeting the requirements under subparagraph (A) cannot be found (or for purposes of applying subsection (b)(2)(B)(i), regardless of whether merchandise meeting such requirements can be found), merchandise that—

"(i) was produced in the same country as, but not produced by the same person as, the merchandise being appraised, and

"(ii) meets the requirement set forth in subparagraph (A)(ii) and (iii).

Such term does not include merchandise that incorporates or reflects any engineering, development, artwork, design work, or plan or sketch that—

"(I) was supplied free or at reduced cost by the buyer of the merchandise for use in connection with the production or the sale for export to the United States of the merchandise; and

"(II) is not an assist because undertaken within the United States

"(5) The term 'sufficient information', when required under this section for determining—

"(A) any amount—

"(i) added under subsection (b)(1) to the price actually paid or payable,

"(ii) deducted under subsection (d)(3) as profit or general expense or value from further processing, or

"(iii) added under subsection (e)(2) as profit or general expense;

"(B) any difference taken into account for purposes of subsection (b)(2)(C); or

"(C) any adjustment made under subsection (c)(2); means information that establishes the accuracy of such amount, difference, or adjustment."

carriers certificate

To the District Director of Customs: _____
_____   (Date)
(Port of entry)

The undersigned carrier, to whom or upon whose order the articles described below or in the attached document must be released,* hereby certifies that _____ of _____ is the owner or consignee of such articles within the purview of section 484(h), Tariff Act of 1930.

Marks and number of packages	Description and quantity of merchandise— Number and kind of packages	Gross weight in pounds	Foreign port of landing and date of sailing	Bill of lading number

Carrier _____   _____
                                                  (Name of carrier)

Voyage No. _____

Arrived _____   _____
             (Date)   (Agent)

*Under the tariff laws of the United States Customs officers do not deliver the goods to the consignee. The goods are released from Customs custody to or upon the order of the carrier by whom the goods are brought to the port at which they are entered for consumption. When the goods are entered for warehouse, they are released from Customs custody to or upon the order of the proprietor of the warehouse.

Department of the Treasury
U. S Customs Service
141.32, C.R.

POWER OF ATTORNEY

Check appropriate box
☐ Individual
☐ Partnership
☐ Corporation
☐ Sole Proprietorship

KNOW ALL MEN BY THESE PRESENTS: That, _____
(Full Name of person, partnership, or corporation, or sole proprietorship (Identify))

a corporation doing business under the laws of the State of _____ or a _____
doing business as _____ residing at _____
having an office and place of business at _____, hereby constitutes and appoints each of the following persons

(Give full name of each agent designated)

as a true and lawful agent and attorney of the grantor named above for and in the name, place, and stead of said grantor from this date and in Customs District _____; and in no other name, to make, endorse, sign, declare, or swear to any entry, withdrawal, declaration, certificate, bill of lading, or other document required by law regulation in connection with the importation, transportation, or exportation of any merchandise shipped or consigned by or to said grantor; to perform any act or condition which may be required by law or regulation in connection with such merchandise; to receive any merchandise deliverable to said grantor;

To make endorsements on bills of lading conferring authority to make entry and collect drawback, and to make, sign, declare, or swear to any statement, supplemental statement, schedule, supplemental schedule, certificate of delivery, certificate of manufacture, certificate of manufacture and delivery, abstract of manufacturing records, declaration of proprietor on drawback entry, declaration of exporter on drawback entry, or any other affidavit or document which may be required by law or regulation for drawback purposes, regardless of whether such bill of lading, sworn statement, schedule, certificate, abstract, declaration, or other affidavit or document is intended for filing in said district or in any other customs district;

To sign, seal, and deliver for and as the act of said grantor any bond required by law or regulation in connection with the entry or withdrawal of imported merchandise or merchandise exported with or without benefit of drawback, or in connection with the entry, clearance, lading, unlading or navigation of any vessel or other means of conveyance owned or operated by said grantor, and any and all bonds which may be

voluntarily given and accepted under applicable laws and regulations, consignee's and owner's declarations provided for in section 485, Tariff Act of 1930, as amended, or affidavits in connection with the entry of merchandise.

To sign and swear to any document and to perform any act that may be necessary or required by law or regulation in connection with the entering, clearing, lading, unlading, or operation of any vessel or other means of conveyance owned or operated by said grantor.

And generally to transact at the customhouses in said district any and all customs business, including making, signing, and filing of protests under section 514 of the Tariff Act of 1930, in which said grantor is or may be concerned or interested and which may properly be transacted or performed by an agent and attorney, giving to said agent and attorney full power and authority to do anything whatever requisite and necessary to be done in the premises as fully as said grantor could do if present and acting, hereby ratifying and confirming all that the said agent and attorney shall lawfully do by virtue of these presents; the foregoing power of attorney to remain in full force and effect until the _____ day of _____, 19___, or until notice of revocation in writing is duly given to and received by the District Director of Customs of the district aforesaid. If the donor of this power of attorney is a partnership, said the power shall in no case have any force or effect after the expiration of 2 years from the date of its receipt in the office of the district director of customs of the said district.

IN WITNESS WHEREOF, the said _____
has caused these presents to be sealed and signed: (Signature) _____
(Capacity) _____ (Date) _____
WITNESS· _____ _____

(Corporate seal) *(Optional)

Customs Form 5291 (10-07-80)

(SEE OVER)

INDIVIDUAL OR PARTNERSHIP CERTIFICATION *(Optional)

CITY_____
COUNTY_____ } ss:
STATE_____

On this _____ day of _____, 19___, personally appeared before me _____

residing at _____, personally known or sufficiently identified to me, who certifies that

_____(is)(are) the individual(s) who executed the foregoing instrument and acknowledge it to be _____ free act and deed.

_____
(Notary Public)

CORPORATE CERTIFICATION *(Optional)
(To be made by an officer other than the one who executes the power of attorney)

I, _____, certify that I am the _____

of _____, organized under the laws of the State of _____

that _____, who signed this power of attorney on behalf of the donor, is the _____

of said corporation; and that said power of attorney was duly signed, sealed, and attested for and behalf of said corporation by authority of its governing body as the

same appears in a resolution of the Board of Directors passed at a regular meeting held on the _____ day of _____, now in my possession or custody. I

further certify that the resolution is in accordance with the articles of incorporation and bylaws of said corporation.

IN WITNESS WHEREOF, I have hereunto set my hand and affixed the seal of said corporation, at the City of _____ this _____ day of

_____, 19 ____

_____   _____
(Signature)   (Date)

If the corporation has no corporate seal, the fact shall be stated, in which case a scroll or adhesive shall appear in the appropriate, designated place.

Customs powers of attorney of residents (including resident corporations) shall be without power of substitution except for the purpose of executing shipper's export declarations. However, a power of attorney executed in favor of a licensed customhouse broker may specify that the power of attorney is granted to the customhouse broker to act through any of its licensed officers or any employee specifically authorized to act for such customhouse broker by power of attorney.

*NOTE· The corporate seal may be omitted. Customs does not require completion of a certification. The grantor has the option of executing the certification or omitting it.

*U.S.GPO:1994-301-616/90746

| 1. THIS FORM MUST BE TYPED.
2. DO NOT ALTER THIS FORM.
3. ORIGINAL TO BE SUBMITTED TO CUSTOMS. (See Option explained in Instruction no. 2) | DEPARTMENT OF THE TREASURY
UNITED STATES CUSTOMS SERVICE
CORPORATE SURETY POWER OF ATTORNEY | Approved through 09/30/95; OMB No. 1515-0144
CUSTOMS USE ONLY
DATE RECEIVED |

☐ GRANT (Instruction No 3a) ☐ CHANGE to Grant on file (Instruction No. 3b.) ☐ REVOCATION. The below-described powers previously granted are hereby revoked. (Instruction No. 3c.)   EFFECTIVE DATE

GRANTEE: NAME   ☐ This is a name change   ADDRESS   ☐ This is an address change

SOCIAL SECURITY NO.

GRANTOR: Surety Company's Corporate Name   Surety No.   State Under Whose laws organized as a surety

District Code(s) for Customs district(s) in which authorized to do business and limit on any single obligation -OR- district(s) being added to the original grant:

District	Limit	District	Limit	District	Limit	District	Limit	District	Limit	District	Limit	District	Limit

Grantor appoints the above-named person (Grantee) as its attorney in fact to sign its name as surety to, and to execute, seal, and acknowledge any bond so as to bind the surety corporation to the same extent as if done by a regularly elected officer, limited only to the extent shown above as to Customs district and amount on any single bond obligation. This grant, or change to a grant on file, or revocation, as specified, shall become active on the effective date shown provided the Customs Form 5297 is received at a district office 5 days before the effective date shown; otherwise the specified action will become active at the close of business 5 working days after the date of receipt at the district office.

| In witness whereof, the said Grantor, by virtue of authority conferred by its Board of Directors, has caused these presents to be sealed with its corporate seal and attested by any two principal officers. | Date Attested

Use a facsimile of corporate seal, and not impression seal. | Name and Title

SIGNATURE: | Name and Title

SIGNATURE: |

Customs Form 5297 (100692)

DEPARTMENT OF THE TREASURY US CUSTOMS SERVICE

DEPARTMENT OF THE TREASURY
UNITED STATES CUSTOMS SERVICE

CUSTOMS BOND

19 CFR Part 113

| CUSTOMS USE ONLY | BOND NUMBER¹ (Assigned by Customs) |
| | FILE REFERENCE |

Execution Date

In order to secure payment of any duty, tax or charge and compliance with law or regulation as a result of activity covered by any condition referenced below, we, the below named principal(s) and surety(ies), bind ourselves to the United States in the amount or amounts, as set forth below.

SECTION I—Select Single Transaction OR Continuous Bond (not both) and fill in the applicable blank spaces

| ☐ SINGLE TRANSACTION BOND | Identification of transaction secured by this bond (e.g., entry no., seizure no., etc.) | Date of transaction | Transaction district & port code |

| ☐ CONTINUOUS BOND | Effective date | This bond remains in force for one year beginning with the effective date and for each succeeding annual period, or until terminated. This bond constitutes a separate bond for each period in the amounts listed below for liabilities that accrue in each period. The intention to terminate this bond must be conveyed within the time period and manner prescribed in the Customs Regulations. |

SECTION II— This bond includes the following agreements.² (Check one box only, except that, 1a may be checked independently or with 1, and 3a may be checked independently or with 3. Line out all other parts of this section that are not used.

Activity Code	Activity Name and Customs Regulations in which conditions codified		Limit of Liability	Activity Code	Activity Name and Customs Regulations in which conditions codified		Limit of Liability
☐ 1	Importer or broker	113.62		☐ 5	Public Gauger	113.67	
☐ 1a	Drawback Payment Refunds	113.65		☐ 6	Wool & Fur Products Labeling Acts Importation (Single Entry Only)	113.68	
☐ 2	Custodian of bonded merchandise	113.63		☐ 7	Bill of Lading (Single Entry Only)	113.69	
	(Includes bonded carriers, freight forwarders, cartmen and lightermen, all classes of warehouses, container station operators)			☐ 8	Detention of Copyrighted Material (Single Entry Only)	113.70	
☐ 3	International Carrier	113.64		☐ 9	Neutrality (Single Entry Only)	113.71	
☐ 3a	Instruments of International Traffic	113.66		☐ 10	Court Costs for Condemned Goods (Single Entry Only)	113.72	
☐ 4	Foreign Trade Zone Operator	113.73					

SECTION III— List below all tradenames or unincorporated divisions that will be permitted to obligate this bond in the principal's name including their Customs Identification Number(s).³ (If more space is needed, use Section III (Continuation) on back of form.)

Importer Number	Importer Name	Importer Number	Importer Name

Total number of importer names listed in Section III

Principal and surety agree that any charge against the bond under any of the listed names is as though it was made by the principal(s).

Principal and surety agree that they are bound to the same extent as if they executed a separate bond covering each set of conditions incorporated by reference to the Customs Regulations into this bond.

If the surety fails to appoint an agent under Title 6, United States Code, Section 7, surety consents to service on the Clerk of any United States District Court or the U.S. Court of International Trade, where suit is brought on this bond. That clerk is to send notice of the service to the surety at.

Mailing Address Requested by the Surety

	Name and Address	Importer No.⁵	
PRINCIPAL⁴		SIGNATURE⁶	**SEAL**
PRINCIPAL⁴	Name and Address	Importer No.⁵	
		SIGNATURE⁶	**SEAL**
SURETY⁴'⁹	Name and Address⁶	Surety No.⁷	
		SIGNATURE⁶	**SEAL**
SURETY⁴'⁹	Name and Address⁶	Surety No.⁷	
		SIGNATURE⁶	**SEAL**
SURETY AGENTS	Name⁸	Identification No.⁹	Name⁸	Identification No.⁹

PART 1-U.S. CUSTOMS

Customs Form 301 (102593)

Note. Turn carbons over before writing on back of form.

SECTION III (Continuation)

Importer Number	Importer Name	Importer Number	Importer Name

WITNESSES

Two witnesses are required to authenticate the signature of any person who signs as an individual or partner; however a witness may authenticate the signatures of both such non-corporate principals and sureties. No witness is needed to authenticate the signature of a corporate official or agent who signs for the corporation.

SIGNED, SEALED, and DELIVERED in the PRESENCE OF:

Name and Address of Witness for the Principal

SIGNATURE:

Name and Address of Witness for the Principal

SIGNATURE:

Name and Address of Witness for the Surety

SIGNATURE:

Name and Address of Witness for the Surety

SIGNATURE:

EXPLANATIONS AND FOOTNOTES

1. The Customs Bond Number is a control number assigned by Customs to the bond contract when the bond is approved by an authorized Customs official.
2. For all bond coverage available and the language of the bond conditions refer to Part 113, subpart G, Customs Regulations.
3. The Importer Number is the Customs identification number filed pursuant to section 24.5, Customs Regulations. When the Internal Revenue Service employer identification number is used the two-digit suffix code must be shown.
4. If the principal or surety is a corporation, the name of the State in which incorporated must be shown.
5. See witness requirement above

6. Surety Name, if a corporation, shall be the company's name as it is spelled in the Surety Companies Annual List published in the Federal Register by the Department of the Treasury (Treasury Department Circular 570).
7. Surety Number is the three digit identification code assigned by Customs to a surety company at the time the surety company initially gives notice to Customs that the company will be writing Customs bonds.
8. Surety Agent is the individual granted a Corporate Surety Power of Attorney, CF 5297, by the surety company executing the bond.
9. Agent Identification No. shall be the individual's Social Security number as shown on the Corporate Surety Power of Attorney, CF 5297, filed by the surety granting such power of attorney.

Customs Form 301 (102593)(Back)

DEPARTMENT OF THE TREASURY
UNITED STATES CUSTOMS SERVICE

ENTRY SUMMARY

Form Approved OMB No. 1515-0065

① Entry No.	② Entry Type Code	③ Entry Summary Date
4. Entry Date	⑤ Port Code	
6. Bond No.	7. Bond Type Code	8. Broker/Importer File No.

9. Ultimate Consignee Name and Address	10. Consignee No.	⑪ Importer of Record Name and Address	⑫ Importer No.
		⑬ Exporting Country	14. Export Date
		⑮ Country of Origin	16. Missing Documents
	State	⑰ I.T. No.	⑱ I.T Date

⑲ B/L or AWB No.	20. Mode of Transportation	21. Manufacturer I.D.	22. Reference No.
㉓ Importing Carrier	24. Foreign Port of Lading	25. Location of Goods/G.O. No.	
26. U.S. Port of Unlading	㉗ Import Date		

㉘ Line No.	30. Ⓐ T.S.U.S.A. No. Ⓑ ADA/CVD Case No.	㉙ Description of Merchandise 31. Ⓐ Gross Weight Ⓑ Manifest Qty.	㉜ Net Quantity in T.S.U.S.A. Units	33. Ⓐ Entered Value Ⓑ CHGS Ⓒ Relationship	34. Ⓐ T.S U.S.A. Rate Ⓑ ADA/CVD Rate Ⓒ I.R.C. Rate Ⓓ Visa No.	㉟ Duty and I.R. Tax Dollars	Cents

㊱ Declaration of Importer of Record (Owner or Purchaser) or Authorized Agent

I declare that I am the
☐ Importer of record and that the actual owner, purchaser, or consignee for customs purposes is as shown above.   **OR**   ☐ owner or purchaser or agent thereof.

I further declare that the merchandise
☐ was obtained pursuant to a purchase or agreement to purchase and that the prices set forth in the invoices are true.   **OR**   ☐ was not obtained pursuant to a purchase or agreement to purchase and the statements in the invoices as to value or price are true to the best of my knowledge and belief.

I also declare that the statements in the documents herein filed fully disclose to the best of my knowledge and belief the true prices, values, quantities, rebates, drawbacks, fees, commissions, and royalties and are true and correct, and that all goods or services provided to the seller of the merchandise either free or at reduced cost are fully disclosed. I will immediately furnish to the appropriate customs officer any information showing a different state of facts.

Notice required by Paperwork Reduction Act of 1980: This information is needed to ensure that importers/exporters are complying with U.S. customs laws, to allow us to compute and collect the right amount of money, to enforce other agency requirements, and to collect accurate statistical information on imports. Your response is mandatory. (Continued on back of form.)

▼ U.S. CUSTOMS USE ▼		TOTALS
A. Liq. Code	B. Ascertained Duty	㊲ Duty
	C. Ascertained Tax	㊳ Tax
	D. Ascertained Other	㊴ Other
	E. Ascertained Total	㊵ Total
㊶ Signature of Declarant, Title, and Date		

5. OTHER AGENCIES (CHAPTERS 29, 30, 31)

U.S. Department of Agriculture

Agricultural Marketing Service
Washington, DC 20250
Tel (202) 720-8998
www.ams.usda.gov

Animal and Plant Health
Inspection Service (APHIS)

Animals
USDA-APHIS-VS
Riverdale, MD 20737–1231
Tel (301) 734-7885

Plants:
USDA-APHIS-PPQ
Riverdale, MD 20737–1231
Tel. (301) 734-8896
www.aphis.usda.gov

Food Safety and Inspection Service
Import Inspection Division
106 South 15th Street
Omaha, NE 68102
Tel. (402) 221-7400

Foreign Agricultural Service
Room 5531-S
Washington, D.C. 20250-1000
Tel. (202) 720-2916
Fax (202) 720-6556
www.usda.gov

U.S. Department of Commerce

Exporter Counseling Division
14th Street & Pennsylvania Ave., N W.
Washington, DC 20230
Tel. (202) 482-4811
www.bxa.doc.gov

National Marine Fisheries Service Headquarters
National Oceanic and Atmospheric Administration
1315 East-West Highway
Silver Spring, MD 20910
Tel. (301) 713-2289

NMFS Southwest Region
Protected Species Management Division
501 West Ocean Blvd.
Long Beach, CA 90802-4213
Tel. (562) 980-4019
www.kingfish.ssp.nms.gov

Federal Communications Commission

Enforcement Division
Investigations Branch, Imports
1919 M Street, NW
Washington, DC 20554
Tel. (202) 418-1170

Office of Engineering and Technology
Washington, DC 20554
Tel. (202) 418-2470
www.fcc.gov

U.S. Consumer Product Safety Commission

Office of Compliance
Washington, DC 20207
Tel (202) 504-0400
www.cpsc.gov

Environmental Protection Agency

Hazardous Materials Hotline
1-800-424-9346

TSCA Assistance Information Service
Tel. (202) 554-1404

Motor Vehicles Investigation/Imports Section (6405-J)
Washington, D.C 20460
Tel. (202) 564-9660

U.S. Department of Health and Human Services

Center for Food Safety and Applied Nutrition

Office of Food Labeling (HFS–156)
200 "C" St., NW
Washington, DC 20204
Tel. (202) 205-5233

Office of Seafood
Washington, DC 20204
Tel. (202) 418-3150

Food and Drug Administration

Center for Biologics Evaluation and Research
1401 Rockville Pike
Suite 200 North
Rockville, MD 20852
Tel (301) 827-6201

Center for Devices and Radiological Health
Rockville, MD 20850
Tel. (301) 594-4692

Division of Import Operations and Policy (HFC–170)
5600 Fishers Lane
Rockville, MD 20857
Tel. (301) 443-6553
Fax (301) 594-0413
www.fda.gov

U.S. Public Health Service

Centers for Disease Control and Prevention
Office of Health and Safety
1600 Clifton Road
Atlanta, Georgia 30333
Tel. (404) 639-3235
www.cdc.gov

U.S. Department of Energy

Office of Codes and Standards
Washington, DC 20585
Tel. (202) 586-9127
www.eren.doe.gov

U.S. Department of the Interior

U.S. Department of the Interior
Fish and Wildlife Service
Office of Management Authority
4401 N. Fairfax Drive
Arlington, VA 22203
Tel. (703) 358-2093
www.fws.gov

U.S. Department of Justice

Drug Enforcement Administration
700 Army-Navy Drive
Arlington VA 22202
Tel. (202) 307-7977
Fax (202) 307-7965
www.usdoj.gov/dea

Nuclear Regulatory Commission

Office of International Programs
One White Flint North
11555 Rockville Pike
Rockville, MD 20852
Tel. (301) 415-7000

Federal Trade Commission

Bureau of Consumer Protection
Washington, DC 20580
Tel. (202) 326-2996

Division of Enforcement
Washington, DC 20580
Tel. (202) 326-2996
www.ftc.gov

International Trade Commission

500 "E" Street, SW
Washington, DC 20436
Tel. (202) 205-2000
www.usitc.gov

U.S. Department of State

Office of Defense Trade Controls
PM/DTC, Room 200, SA-6
Bureau of Political/Military Affairs
Washington, DC 20522-0602
Tel. (703) 875-6644
www.pmdtc.org

U.S. Department of Transportation

National Highway Traffic Safety Administration
Office of Vehicle Safety Compliance (NEF-32)
400 7th Street SW
Washington, DC 20590
Tel. 1-800-424-9393
Fax (202) 366-1024
www.nhtsa.dot.gov

Boating Standards Branch
U.S. Coast Guard
Commandant (G-NAB-6)
Washington, DC 20593
Tel. (202) 276-0985

Office of Hazardous Materials
400 7th Street SW
Washington, DC 20590-0001
Tel. (202) 366-4488

U.S. Department of the Treasury

Bureau of Alcohol, Tobacco, and Firearms
Washington, DC 20226
Tel. (202) 927-7920 (arms and ammunition)
    (202) 927-8110 (alcoholic beverages)
www.atf.treas.gov

U.S. Customs Service

    Office of Regulations and Rulings
    1300 Pennsylvania Avenue NW
    Washington, DC 20229
    Tel. (202) 927-0760

    National Import Specialist Division
    6 World Trade Center
    New York, NY 10048
    Tel. (212) 466-5618
    Fax (212) 466-5830
www.customs.ustreas.gov

Office of Foreign Assets Control
1500 Pennsylvania Avenue NW
Washington, DC 20220
Tel. (202) 622-2500
Fax (202) 622-1657

U.S. Secret Service
Washington, DC 20223
Tel. (202) 435-5708
www.tre.gov/treasury/bureaus/usss
www.treas.gov/treasury/services/fac

Printed in the United States
15917LVS00001B/87